Birutė Imbrasienė

Traditional Lithuanian
Lenten
Meals

Birutė Imbrasienė

baltos lankos

UDK 641.56(083)
Tr-09

This book presents recipes for traditional meatless dishes
that belong to the Lithuanian culinary heritage.

Compiled by Birutė Imbrasienė
Translated into English by Jonas Steponaitis
Edited by Jayde Will
Designer: Agnė Dautartaitė-Krutulienė
Photographers: Karlas (Artūras Moisiejenko);
          Henrikas Sakalauskas

ISBN 9955-23-007-X

CONTENTS

LITHUANIAN MEALS
AND EATING HABITS / 9 /

potatoes

Steamed Potatoes in their Skins /88/
Stewed Potatoes /88/
Boiled Potatoes in their Skins /88/
Potatoes in their Skins Stuffed
with Herring /88/
Potatoes Stuffed with Fish /89/
Potatoes Stuffed with Mushrooms /89/
Grated Potatoes (Kugel, Potato Pudding) /89/
Grated Potatoes with Buckwheat /90/
Grated Potatoes with Poppy Seeds
or Hemp Seed /90/
Grated Potatoes with Dried Mushrooms /90/
Grated Potato Cold Noses /90/
Grated Potatoes with Yeast /91/
Potato Dumplings /91/
Žemaičių Potato /93/
Dumplings with Cottage Cheese and
Poppy Seeds /93/
Potato Pasties with Hemp Seed Curd /94/
Potatoes Stewed in Butter /94/
Stewed Potatoes and Mushrooms /94/
Stewed Potatoes, Mushrooms, and
Sauerkraut /95/
Stewed Potatoes /95/
Herring, and Sauerkraut /95/
Stewed Potatoes and Fish in
Mushroom Sauce /95/
Stewed Potatoes and Herring /96/
Stewed Potatoes /96/
Potatoes with Peas /96/
Potatoes with Broad Beans /97/
Potatoes with Sauerkraut /97/
Baked Mashed Potatoes with Mushrooms /97/
Baked Potatoes with Sauerkraut /97/
Baked Mashed Potatoes with Cabbage /98/
Baked Potatoes with Herring /98/
Potato Roll with Sauerkraut and
Mushrooms /98/
Half-and-Half Porridge /99/
Potato Porridge /99/
Mashed Potatoes with Seeds /99/
Lenten Fat /99/
Dry Mashed Potatoes /100/
Mashed Potatoes with Cottage Cheese /100/
Mashed Potatoes with Mushrooms /100/
Potatoes and Mushroom Croquettes /100/
Potato Croquettes with
Mushroom Sauce /102/
Potato Turnovers with Cottage Cheese
Filling /102/
Potato Rolls with Cottage Cheese /102/
Baked Potato Pasties

"Wooden Spoons"/103/
Marmots /104/
Potato Rings with Fish /104/
Potato Rings with Cottage Cheese /104/
Potato Dumplings in
Mushroom Sauce /105/
Potato Dumplings with Poppy Seeds /105/
Mashed Potato Pancakes with
Mushrooms /105/
Potato Pancakes /106/
Potato Pancakes with
Cottage Cheese /106/
Potato Pancakes Baked on
Cabbage Leaves /106/
Potato Pancakes with Poppy Seeds /108/
Grated and Boiled
Potatoes Pancakes /108/
Cottage Cheese Buns with
Grated Potatoes /108/
Potato Pancakes with Yeast /108/
Potato Pancakes with
Buckwheat Flour /109/
Potato Buns /109/
Potato Bowls /109/
Potato Dumplings /109/
Potato Porridge /111/
Potato Porridge with Buckwheat /111/
Potato Porridge with Caraway Seeds /111/
Potatoes Baked with Cheese /111/
Baked Potatoes with Cheese /112/
Potatoes Stewed in Whey /112/
Potatoes with Hemp Seed /112/
Potatoes in Sauce /112/
Sauces Served with Potatoes /114/

milk

Lithuanian Farmer's Cheese /120/
Sour Cream Butter /120/
Sour Cheese /120/
Sour Cheese with Caraway Seeds /122/
Sour Cheese with Poppy Seeds /122/
Sour Cheese with Mint /122/
Sour Cheese with Seasonings /122/
Sour Cheese with Mushrooms /122/
Sour Cheese with Garlic /123/
Baked Cottage Cheese Cakes /123/
Seasoned Butter /123/
Butter with Garlic and Cheese /123/
Cottage Cheese with Sour Cream /123/
Cottage Cheese with Garlic /125/
Cottage Cheese with Tarragon /125/
Cottage Cheese with Bread /125/
Boiled Cottage Cheese Dumplings /125/

Cottage Cheese Dumplings /126/
Colostrum /126/
Colostrum Pancakes /126/
Cheese with Cream /126/
Cheese Rolled in Egg/129/
Baked Farmer's Cheese/129/
Baked Cheese with Mint/129/
Cheese Wrapped in Pastry/129/
Baked Dried Cheese/129/
Buttermilk with Onions /130/
Baked Cottage Cheese /130/
Cottage Cheese /130/
Patties with Potato /130/
Cottage Cheese /130/
Dumplings with Bread /130/
Cottage Cheese Squares with
Buckwheat /131/
Cottage Cheese Casserole
with Carrot /131/
Hedgehogs /131/

mushrooms

Fried Mushrooms with Onions /134/
Fried Saffron Milkcaps with Onions /134/
Mushroom Caps Fried in Butter /134/
Mushroom and Potato Stew /134/
Stewed Mushrooms with Sour Cream /135/
Batter-Fried Mushrooms /135/
Mushrooms in Sauce /135/
Fried Dried Mushrooms /135/
Mushroom Sauce /136/
Mushroomers' Roast /136/
Salted Mushroom Patties /136/
Ears with Mushroom Filling /136/
Mushroom Cake /138/
King Bolete Cheese /138/
Mushrooms in Eggs /138/
Fresh Mushrooms with Herring /139/
Mushroom Omelette /139/
Baked Mushrooms with Bread /139/
Baked Mushrooms with Buckwheat /141/
Mushroom Salad /141/
Chanterelle Stew /141/
Fried Chanterelles /141/

fish

Dried Smelt and Other Small Fish /144/
Salted Vimba /144/
Salted Bleak with Yellow Knight
Mushrooms /144/
Fried Crucian Carp /145/
Baked Eel /145/
Baked Trout Stuffed with

LITHUANIAN MEALS AND EATING HABITS

Lithuanians like delicious and satisfying meals. This quality has been inherited from their ancestors, and even Lithuanian folk wisdom says: "Eat until you burst, work to inspire envy", for only he who eats well works well.

Lithuanian homemakers prepare simple, healthy and delicious meals. They use a wide variety of foods because for centuries Lithuania has grown various grains, bred livestock, fish, kept bees, vegetable gardens, and orchards, and gathered food provided by the forest.

Throughout their history Lithuanians have been a nation of farmers and have mainly tilled the soil, so grain occupies an important place in their traditional diet and customs. Along with this, the bounty of the forest, vegetables, fish and dairy products have been used by Lithuanians also. Created to present traditional Lithuanian food, this book does not include meat dishes, which make up a substantial part of Lithuanian traditional cooking.

According to tradition, the mother has always prepared the food for the family. She passes her experience and skills on to her daughters so that they would be good cooks and hosts.

Even in today's kitchen, homemakers cook and bake many foods, learning secrets from their mothers and grandmothers. Although they use many of the same ingredients, homemakers today are influenced less by the seasonalness of food than they were just a quarter of a century ago. Now they have access to fresh (home-grown or imported) vegetables, fruits, spices, and herbs all year round.

Even today we appreciate the adage that "a good cook can make a meal out of nothing", and we understand that the taste and variety of meals depend on the resourcefulness and inventiveness of the one cooking. Thus, "each cook stirs the pot differently".

Traditional Lithuanian cuisine has been formed over the centuries and has been influenced by cultural relations with neighbors. However, the national cuisine of Lithuania does not have many dishes coming from outside Lithuania. This is because Lithuanians distinguish themselves with their conservatism. Innovations are regarded with caution and distrust, and are observed for a long period of time before people get used to them and adapt them. People living in rural areas often chide city people for their greater openness to new things: "What their lordships eat, sometimes even a pig won't touch." When they accept something as suitable and adapt it to their taste, they consider it their own and do not let it go. As an example, kugelis (kugel, or potato pudding), which was borrowed from German cuisine, is now very popular throughout Lithuania, and is considered a traditional dish.

Although Lithuania is not large, different ethnographic regions have developed different diets and have different food preferences. The people from the Žemaitija region in western Lithuania like sour cream butter, porridge, and vegetable soup, while those of Aukštaitija in northeast Lithuania like pancakes and cottage cheese. People from the Dzūkija region in southeastern Lithuania like foods from buckwheat, mushrooms, and potatoes, and those of the Suvalkija region in southwestern Lithuania like potato dumplings and potato sausages, while people living along the seashore like fish dishes.

These differences, which are now less clear-cut, were determined not only by respect for tradition but also by natural conditions – buckwheat grows in sandy soil, and wheat grows in black soil rich in humus. People in well-forested areas have gathered berries and mushrooms for centuries, while those living near the sea and large rivers and lakes consume more various kinds of fish.

Lithuanians usually eat three times a day, having breakfast, lunch, and dinner. Additional meals are also eaten in the late morning and late afternoon, but not always and not in all families. This custom depends on the type of work, age, and habits of family members.

Formerly, particular foods were prepared for each part of the day. People used to eat most heartily at breakfast (porridge, pancakes, and soups) and at lunch (soups, potatoes, mushrooms, and other satisfying dishes). For dinner there were light foods (milk soup, potatoes with sour milk).

Lithuanians have maintained a tradition of healthy and well-balanced nutrition. Even today, they eat the most at breakfast and lunch. Quick but satisfying meals are usually prepared for breakfast, such as boiled or fried eggs, pancakes, or porridge. Some families, however, especially in rural areas, still follow the tradition of having soup for breakfast. This traditional menu has mainly been preserved by the middle and older generations. Foods served at dinner have departed the least from the traditional menu. In the evening people eat lightly, but they do not go to bed without eating, because if you lie down without having eaten – you will get up without having slept.

The main courses at breakfast, lunch, and dinner are prepared fresh and served hot, with cold dishes only complementing them.

Lithuanians consider eating a special and holy event. It is said: "At the table is like being in church." Therefore, the behavior at the table is quiet, orderly and reverential. This order has been held sacred by entire generations and has been taught to the youngest children. Thus the rich eating customs and etiquette have survived until today.

In earlier times, a linen tablecloth was spread on the table for each meal. Each member of the family had his or her permanent place. The master of the household was at the head of the table against the wall and to his right was the oldest son. Beside him were the other men, and the women were along the other side of the table opposite the men. The mistress was at the other end of the table opposite the master of the household.

Even today, when putting food on the table and while eating, people follow the traditional order and customs. The bread is put on the table first. It cannot be put on the table upside down because doing so would be an act of desecration. After the bread is sliced, the knife cannot be left with its blade facing upward because anyone born that minute will have a conflicting character. The end of the sliced bread is given to that person who wishes the birth of a son.

If someone from outside the family arrives during a meal, he traditionally enters with a greeting, such as "God grant you abundance", "Abundance", "Have a delicious meal", or "Enjoy your meal". He is answered "Please" or "Thank you". If the host answers "Please" that means that the guest is being invited to sit down at the table, but if they answer only "Thank you", then he is not permitted to approach the table.

Nowadays, the customary order for being seated at the table is not usually followed because all the members of a family gather only during traditional holidays.

A linen tablecloth no longer covers the table for each daily meal, but there is certainly one whenever a guest is being entertained or the family is celebrating a holiday.

For Lithuanians, the most important holiday is Kūčios, or Christmas Eve (December 24). This is celebrated at home with a traditional family dinner. In the customs of Christmas Eve, the table plays a special role: here, at this one time during the year the entire family gathers, the living and the dead. On Christmas Eve, therefore, the food not cleared away after eating: it is left on the table overnight. This very old custom symbolizes that the spirits of dead members of the family return home on this night, communicate with us, and feast on the same food. Therefore, in order to please these spirits, their favorite foods are prepared. The traditional foods of Christmas Eve are those of a fast. The most important dish is kūčia. This very old word, which is common to many European languages, was borrowed by Lithuanians in the 12th century from the Slavs, who in turn had borrowed it from the ancient Greeks (the Greek word kukkia has the same meaning). Kūčia is a dish made from cereal grains grown by our ancestors since olden times – boiled barley, rye, beans, peas, and oats mixed with miešimas (water sweetened with honey) – and intended primarily for the spirits of ancestors invited to the feast. It is a sacrificial dish eaten by those making the sacrifice. This dish gives its name to the ritual dinner and to the holiday itself. Only once a year, for Kūčios, little wheat-dough pastries – kūčiukai – are baked and eaten with poppy seed milk. A very old and essential Kūčios dish is avižinis kisielius (oat pudding), which is eaten with sweetened water. Beet soup with mushrooms is made, and fish (especially herring and pike) and mushroom dishes are prepared. Apples and nuts are also put on the table. The traditional drinks during Kūčios are cranberry kisielius (kisiel, a tart juice drink) and a compote of dried fruit, both of which are boiled with starch until it is thick. For Kūčios, a range of dishes are prepared, usually numbering seven, nine, or twelve Usually there are twelve because there should be a separate dish on the table for each month to ensure that the coming year is one of abundance.

SOUPS

Lithuanians have soup every day. It is their main food at lunch, but it is also often made for dinner. Formerly, soup also used to be made for breakfast. People have hearty soups for lunch and easily digested and milk-based ones for dinner. Throughout Lithuania, the most popular soups are made with sauerkraut, pickled beets, and sorrel. Many soups are eaten with potatoes or bread.

In winter, soups are often made from sauerkraut or beets, and in spring and summer – from nettles, sorrel, young beet stems, and milk. In summer, cold beet soup (šaltibarščiai) is often made. There are many different recipes, and it is eaten with hot potatoes. In summer, people (especially in Suvalkija) also used to make sweet fruit or berry soups that are still popular today. Yet another summertime soup is mutinys, or bread soup. It is made by pouring water over crumbled bread and sweetened with honey or sugar. Crushed fresh berries or preserves are then added to the mixture.

Roughly until the early 20th century, Lithuanian homemakers used neither vinegar nor citric acid. They made sour soups from sauerkraut, pickles, pickled beets, and sorrel, or they added tart apples, beet brine, whey, and fermented tree sap.

GRAIN

The oldest and most important Lithuanian food product is grain. For centuries, the people of our country have grown various kinds of cereal (rye, wheat, barley, oats, buckwheat, peas, broad beans) and oil-bearing cultures (hemp seed, linseed, poppy seeds). Of these grains, the most important is rye, from which bread is baked and other foods are made. Buckwheat is grown in eastern Aukštaitija and in the hilly parts of Dzūkija, where it is also mainly used. Of the oil-bearing cultures, the most popular in traditional cooking are linseed, hemp seed, and poppy seeds. Many dishes are made with hemp seed in Žemaitija, and with poppy seeds in Dzūkija.

As the main source of food, the grain harvest determined the prosperity of the people. Therefore, in order to reap a bountiful harvest, Lithuanians, like other people who tilled the soil, followed long-standing customs. They used to say: "Do not go into the field to sow on an empty stomach, because then the ears of grain will also be empty."

Groats have been known in Lithuania for centuries. Until the late 19th century they were ground by hand using a mortar and pestle. Nowadays, store-bought groats are mainly used. Porridges are made from groats. Porridges are most popular among the people of Žemaitija. After filling himself with porridge, one will not say that his "ribs are sticking to each other". Pancakes are a very old food. Made in many different ways, they are the traditional breakfast food of Aukštaitija. Today, throughout Lithuania, people mainly use rye and wheat flour. In Dzūkija, traditionally popular are dishes with buckwheat groats and flour. In Aukštaitija, people like foods made with peas and pea flour.

The main Lithuanian food is rye bread. It is eaten every day at breakfast, lunch, and dinner. For this reason, bread occurs in folklore as a symbol of all food. Many customs, beliefs, and superstitions are connected with bread. It is used in the rituals of family holidays and in the ceremonies of agrarian festivals. Magical qualities are ascribed to bread: it is put into the foundation when a new home is built to protect it against fire.

Traditional Lithuanian bread is of two kinds; plain (or leavened) and hot water. Plain black bread has been baked in Lithuania for centuries, while the baking of hot water bread began only in the early 20th century.

Bread is baked in an oven heated with firewood. In earlier times there was an oven for baking bread in every farmhouse. For centuries, baking bread has been an honorable duty of the wife and mother. In a special ritual, she used to pass this duty on to her grown daughter.

The customs of our nation show that Lithuanians had an extraordinary reverence for bread. The day when bread was baked was considered special. The home had to be calm: quarreling was not allowed. A special word – užkeptas – described someone who arrived while bread was being baked, and this guest had to wait until the baking was finished. A piece of freshly baked bread had to be given to the chance visitor for his journey. On that day nothing from the house could be loaned, because the borrower would carry out the abundance of the bread.

Today Lithuanians have forgotten many old customs, but they always value their bread and take pride in its taste. They understand that one's own bread is more delicious than someone else's cake. Many no longer bake their own bread, but they cherish the traditional belief that bread is more precious than gold, and they teach their children love and respect for bread.

VEGETABLES AND FRUITS

Traditionally Lithuanians have mainly consumed cabbage, beets, carrots, cucumbers, rutabagas, onions, turnips, and radishes. They eat cabbage fresh or pickled with seasonings. Fresh beets are used in preparing dishes. They are also pickled and keep for almost a whole year. People eat cucumbers fresh in summer and pickled in fall and winter. Onions are the main traditional potherb. People also use dill, caraway seeds, garlic, horseradish, parsley, celery, and leeks.

Many Lithuanian farms have orchards and gardens apple, pear, plum, and cherry trees as well as currant and gooseberry bushes. The bounty of the forest is also gathered: raspberries, wild strawberries, lingonberries, blueberries, cranberries, and nuts.

Fruits, berries, and some vegetables are seasonal products. In order for them to be available throughout the year, they are preserved and stored. Lithuanian homemakers like this work and strive to prepare as many seasonal products as possible for their families. To do so, they use both traditional technologies (drying, pickling, and salting) and new, modern ones (canning, marinating, and freezing).

Drying is the oldest and simplest way of preparing stores of fruits, berries, and vegetables. It is done naturally by spreading them out in a thin layer or hanging them up in a dry, well-ventilated place or oven. Not all fruits and berries are dried in an oven at the same temperature: juicy berries and stone fruits are first dried at a low temperature that is gradually increased once they have partially dried. Harder fruits are first dried at a higher temperature that is later decreased. Before being dried, fruits and berries are suitably prepared. Cherries, blueberries, raspberries, black currants, wild strawberries, and rosehips are first picked over. The berries are then spread out in a thin layer and dried in a well-ventilated room where they are protected against the direct rays of the sun or in an oven at a temperature no higher than 30–35 °C while being stirred. Apples are cut into slices, and the seed pouches are removed. Pears are dried without being sliced; only the bigger ones are cut in half. On screens, baking pans, straw or paper, apples and pears are first dried at 75–80 °C, then the drying is finished at a temperature of about 50 °C. Dried berries and fruit are poured into cloth bags and kept in a dry, well-ventilated room.

Some vegetables and wild herbs are salted: sorrel and nettles; leaves from celery, parsley, and dill; stems from beets; and roots from celery and parsley. These vegetables are cleaned, chopped, sprinkled with salt, and pressed together in containers that are tied together tightly or sealed.

Cucumbers, cabbages, beets, apples, and tomatoes are pickled.

POTATOES

Potatoes are a very important food. Historical records show that Lithuanians began to grow them quite recently, only in the 18th century, but potatoes spread very quickly, and in the 19th century they were already widely used alongside turnips and grain for food and animal feed and later on in industry. If one may judge from the borrowed names for them, potatoes came to Lithuania either from the Germans or from the Slavs (bulvė, bulbė, bulba, bulva, kartoklė, kunodai). Other names were taken from those of similar plants.

Today potatoes are grown on every farm. They have become a daily food, the second bread, and are eaten throughout the year. Lithuanians make a great variety of satisfying foods from them, especially from grated potatoes. Somewhat lighter are dishes from boiled potatoes. Many kinds of fillings, sidedishes, and sauces are served with potatoes as main courses. Boiled, baked, or mashed potatoes are also eaten with various other dishes.

MILK

Lithuanians have traditionally used only cow's milk for food, although poor people also used to consume goat's milk. Now goat's milk is returning to the diet of an entirely different social stratum as a source of health. Foods from milk have been known for centuries. According to linguists, this fact is confirmed by some very old Lithuanian words: pienas (milk), krekenos (colostrum), kastinys (sour cream butter), varškė (curd, cottage cheese), sviestas (butter), sūris (cheese), grietinė (cream, sour cream), and išrūgos (whey).

Lithuanians consume milk and milk products every day. They consume both sweet and sour milk, add it to soups, and make cottage cheese, cheese, and butter. Milk products are popular throughout Lithuania. However, people in different regions like some milk products more than others: in Aukštaitija they prefer foods made from cottage cheese, in Žemaitija they make kastinys, a distinctive kind of butter, from a little bit of butter mixed into sour cream with various seasonings. This very old traditional food is widespread only in Žemaitija, where it is still popular today.

Farmer's cheese is the most popular cheese throughout Lithuania. Sweet or sour, it is made by curdling heated milk. It can be marbled, made with caraway seeds, mint, or raisins, and soft or dried. Although regional differences are no longer as clear-cut as they once were (having been influenced by commercial products and imports), the people of Aukštaitija, Žemaitija, Dzūkija, and Suvalkija can still, even today, seriously disagree about how cheese should taste.

The people of Aukštaitija prefer farmer's cheese made from naturally soured milk. The soured milk is slowly warmed and poured into a sieve lined with cheese cloth. After the whey has drained off, salt and sometimes caraway seeds are added, and everything is mixed well. This curd is put into a cheese bag and pressed. Sometimes enriched sour cheese is also made: curdled milk is poured into a cheese bag, squeezed a bit, drained, and shaken out into a bowl. Then some cream is added, everything is mixed and poured back into the cheese bag. This kind of cheese is rich and delicious. When sliced, it does not crumble, and when dried, it breaks easily into pieces. Cheeses made from sour milk are consumed both fresh and dried. While drying, the cheese ripens, becomes crumbly, and acquires a distinctive but pleasant flavor. Dried cheeses are sometimes also smoked.

In Žemaitija, cheese from sour and sweet milk is very popular and has been made for centuries. To make this kind of cheese, sweet whole milk is heated over a low flame. When the sweet milk comes to a boil, an equal amount of sour milk is added. The curdled mass is poured into a cheese bag, and pressed. Instead of caraway seeds, raisins are added and the colour is improved by adding an egg yolk. Curd cheese is made twice so that it will last longer. The cheese made the first time is finely crumbled and added to heated sweet milk. After curdling, the whey is poured off, salt is added along with caraway seeds instead of raisins, and the cheese is pressed.

The people of Žemaitija are most famous for their sweet cheese, which travellers praised in earlier times. To make this kind of cheese, it is necessary to have rennet. A 10–15 cm² piece is put into 10 liters of sweet whole milk which has been salted to taste and is heated while being vigorously stirred until it curdles.

This curdled milk is poured into a cheese bag and drained. After draining, it is poured into a large colander. The next day this cheese mass is turned upside down and kept a while longer until the whey completely drains off. Later, it is put into a wooden form with holes on the bottom or onto a wooden board and kept this way for at least half a year while it ages. To prevent the ripening cheese from becoming mouldy, it is washed once a month with hops tea.

In Suvalkija, people like sour and semi-sweet cheeses made from sour and sweet milk.

Every homemaker makes a different cheese, even from the same recipe. First of all, the fat content and other characteristics of the milk are different. Also, the quality of the milk is determined by the utensils used and the conditions under which it is kept and processed. Most important, however, are the homemaker's intuition and skill, the choice of seasonings, how much is used, and in what proportions. The traditional seasonings added to dairy products are tarragon, mint, oregano, caraway seeds, garlic, onions, parsley, dill, and chives. A good and delicious cheese is a homemaker's pride, because cheese has traditionally been served to esteemed guests; it is brought as a gift for one's host and is given to a departing guest.

Even today, the technology for making cheese remains similar to what it was at the beginning of the last century, but now rennet is very rarely added when making sweet cheese. Sweet cheeses are pressed but not aged because they are soon eaten, while those made from sour milk are sometimes also dried and smoked. Cheeses are pressed with traditional cheese presses and dried in hanging baskets. With equal success, traditional cheese bags are also used.

Today, not only are delicious cheeses and other dairy products made at home, but industrial plants now also follow their recipes.

MUSHROOMS

Lithuania is a country rich in mushrooms. About 400 edible species grow in her forests. However, cooks traditionally use only those mushrooms to which everyone is accustomed. The most valuable mushrooms are considered to be the king bolete (baravykas, Boletus edulis), orange aspen bolete (raudonviršis, Leccinum aurantiacum), brown birch bolete (lepšė, Leccinum scabrum), chanterelle (voveraitė, Cantharellus), brittlegill (ūmėdė, Russula), slippery jack (kazlėkas, Suillus luteus), yellow knight (žaliuokė, Tricholoma equestre), honey mushroom (kelmutis, Armillaria mellea), false morel (bobausis, Gyromitra esculenta), morel (briedžiukas, Morchella), saffron milkcap (rudmėsė, Lactarius deliciosus), and weeping bolete (šilinis baravykas, Suillus granulatus). There are also mushrooms of little value, but few people gather them.

In Lithuania, mushrooms grow from early spring to late autumn, the season when they are the most plentiful. Thus, towards autumn whole families of mushroomers (especially from the cities) pour into the forests. They return with full baskets and without fail count up how many king boletes each of them found. The forests of Dzūkija are the most bountiful for mushroom collectors. Thus, the people there have long since been unsurpassed at gathering mushrooms, and the the best at preparing them. The forests of Lithuania have always had an abundance of diverse mushrooms. Throughout Lithuania freshly picked mushrooms are baked, boiled, roasted on coals, and immediately eaten. When mushrooms are in season, the people of Dzūkija eat them every day. Without mushrooms, breakfast is not a real breakfast, and lunch is not a real lunch.

The traditional ways of preparing supplies of mushrooms are drying, salting, and pickling. The oldest and most popular way is drying. All kinds of mushrooms can be dried, but the most valuable ones are, of course, king boletes. Select fresh, firm mushrooms for drying. Clean off the dirt, needles, and leaves, wipe the mushrooms, but do not wash them. Select mushrooms of roughly uniform size, and cut the bigger ones in half. It is necessary to do so for them to dry out at the same time. Mushrooms are usually dried in an oven, or during a hot and dry summer in the heat of the sun. Skewer the mushrooms on wooden sticks, or string them up on threads that are stretched out on racks. It is important that the mushrooms not touch the walls or bottom of the oven and that they are not squeezed together. They may also be dried in pans lined with straw. If they are dried in an oven, the door should be slightly open so that the moisture evaporating from the mushrooms can escape. It is recommended that at first the mushrooms be briefly heated at 60–70 °C and then dried at a lower temperature (40–45 °C). If they are dried at a higher temperature, the colour, taste, and smell of the mushrooms deteriorate. Mushrooms dry out in 14–24 hrs. (depending on their size). Properly dried mushrooms become light. When bent, they slowly give and break but do not crumble.

It is important not only to dry mushrooms well but also to keep them properly once dried. Dried mushrooms should be picked over and sorted. Put the nicely dried ones into cloth bags, and hang in a dry, warm place so that they do not become damp. Grind the small and crumbly mushrooms, and put in tightly closed jars. It is convenient not only to keep ground mushrooms in this way but also to use them to add flavor to sauces, soups, and other dishes. The homemakers of Dzūkija have kept inferior mushrooms in this way for a long time. Dried mushrooms are used to flavor sour soups (made from sauerkraut or pickled beets) and potato soup. They are the main ingredient of some dishes and are used to add flavor to others.

Another traditional way of storing mushrooms is pickling. This is very popular even today. All mushrooms can be pickled. Different species can be pickled separately or mixed together. Clean off the mushrooms, wash the places gnawed by slugs, and wash well. Then put the mushrooms into a pot, add cold water, and heat to boiling. When the water comes to a boil, stir gently, and skim off the foam that has formed. Boil king boletes, orange aspen boletes, brown birch boletes, and slippery jacks for 10 min. Boil chanterelles and honey mushrooms, for up to half an hour. Then pour the mushrooms into a colander, and drain. Those that have milky juices should be washed again with cold water. Put the mushrooms into wooden barrels, earthenware crocks, or enamel or glass jars in layers 5–7 cm thick. Sprinkle each layer with salt and seasonings (garlic, currant leaves, dill sprigs, caraway seeds). In eastern Lithuania some homemakers also add cranberries or pickle mushrooms together with cabbage. When the container is full, sprinkle seasonings and salt on top, cover with cheese cloth and a lid, and press down firmly. Keep in a cool place.

Mushrooms that have bitter juices – the peppery milk cap (grūzdas, Lactarius piperatus), fleecy milk cap (paliepė, Lactariusvellerius), woolly milk cap (pūkuotė, Lactarius torminosus), etc. – are pickled without boiling. Soak these mushrooms unsliced for 2–3 days. Sort them first, clean off, and add cold water, which should be changed twice a day. Soak the mushrooms until there is no longer any bitterness, and take care they do not begin to ferment. After soaking, put the mushrooms into a wooden keg or earthenware, glass, or enamel container with their caps facing upward in layers of 5–7 cm, each of which should be sprinkled with salt and seasonings (garlic, dill, bay leaves). When the container is full, sprinkle seasonings on top, put on a lid, and press down firmly. Mushrooms prepared this way should be kept in a cool room and can be used at least a month and a half. The mushrooms in the container should always be covered with liquid. If mould appears on the surface, remove it, and wash the cheesecloth, lid, and edges of the container with hot salty water.

For salting, mushrooms are prepared in the same way as for pickling, only more salt is used (for a kilogram of fresh mushrooms 5 tbsps of salt). Then the mushrooms do not ferment or get mouldy but are only salted. Before preparing them to be eaten, first soak the mushrooms several times in water. After a good soaking, salted mushrooms become like fresh, neither sour nor salty. They can be added to soups, made into separate dishes, or used to flavor other foods. Lithuanians are very fond of salted saffron milkcaps, yellow knights, fleecy milkcaps, and peppery milkcaps.

How mushroom dishes taste depends on how they are prepared. It is said: "If you don't spare sour cream and butter when preparing mushrooms, you won't be able to tell a king bolete from a brown birch bolete."

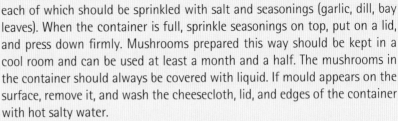

FISH

For those Lithuanians who live near the sea, lagoons, or one of a multitude of lakes and rivers and who live from fishing ,fish have traditionally been one of the most important foods. Today, many fresh water fish are consumed in eastern Lithuania with their abundance of lakes. However, only in the families of fishermen living near by sea fish is a traditional daily food with traditional fish processing technologies safeguarded and maintained.

EGGS

For Lithuanians, eggs were not a daily food, even though eggs and dishes prepared from them are now eaten almost every day. Centuries ago the egg was a symbol of life, goodness, abundant harvests, fruitfulness, and the re-birth of nature as well as a magical means of awakening the forces of life for Lithuanians and many other nations. Thus, it is associated with spring and the holidays of spring for which eggs are dyed and decorated. The custom of dyeing eggs during these holidays is very old and is known to almost all the nations of the Old World. Lithuanians have preserved this custom and continue to cultivate it. During the holidays of spring, especially Easter, dyed eggs are eaten, given as gifts, rolled, and exchanged. Thus, in every home eggs are dyed, and every family tries to dye and decorate them as beautifully as possible, with everyone joining in to help.

There are two traditional ways of decorating eggs in Lithuania: scratching an egg dyed in one colour and drawing a pattern on an egg with hot wax. Scratching designs is a very popular way of decorating Easter eggs. On the surface of an egg dyed in one colour, designs are scratched with a sharp pointed object. The most elaborate and elegant way of decorating a boiled egg consists of drawing a pattern with hot wax. The sharpened end of a matchstick or the head of a pin is dipped into hot wax, and a pattern is drawn. Then the egg is carefully put into a strong dye that has cooled off (if it is put into a hot one, the wax will melt off, and the design will fade) and kept there until the dye takes. The dye takes only in the places not covered with wax, and under the wax, which is later cleaned off, the design remains.

The most popular way of dyeing eggs is with onion peels. A moistened egg is wrapped in them and then in a rag, tied with a string, and boiled in blue, green, or red dye. When dyed in this way, each egg is decorated differently. These unexpected patterns are very popular with children.

A colourful Easter egg is a good decoration on a holiday table. That the egg is a holiday food is also shown by a continuing tradition: even today, a fried egg dish is often prepared when unexpected guests arrive.

BEVERAGES

For Lithuanians, the traditional and ceremonial beverages are mead and beer, of which. Mead is the oldest. In the 11th century, the mead that Lithuanians and Prussians made was already written about by chroniclers and travellers. In olden times, mead was made from the honey of wild bees, later – from that of domestic bees. For centuries, mead was the most important beverage at every feast. Mead aged for ten or more years was the pride of the host, because the longer it is aged, the better the quality. For this reason, whenever a baby was born, the father often made some mead and kept it for the wedding of his son or daughter. In Lithuania, mead was almost displaced by vodka. Thirty years ago, a distillery in Stakliškės began to make this beverage again according to the recipes of our forebears. Mead is now returning to our tables when we entertain guests.

Beer has been made in Lithuania for many centuries, and today it is the most popular traditional beverage. Throughout Lithuania, people drink beer produced in modern breweries, and only in northern Lithuania are the traditions still alive of making homemade beer from barley malt. There, almost every farm still has a complete inventory of supplies for making beer. For holidays and family occasions, the man of the house makes the beer himself, and for weddings, baptisms, funerals, commemorations of the dead, and other big gatherings, when a great deal of especially good beer is needed, a known brewer is called upon. It is also his duty to make sure that the pitchers on the table are full while entertaining guests.

Homemade wine from various wild and garden berries and fruits was first-produced in Lithuania only in the early 20th century. It was mainly made by the people of Suvalkija. Homemade wine is not popular in Lithuania. Efforts are being made to replace it with imports or wine made in Lithuanian wineries. An old Lithuanian beverage is birch or maple sap, which is tapped in early spring before the trees are in leaf. People drink it fresh and ferment it for the summer. Lithuanians also make various kinds of kvass to refresh themselves. For many centuries people have treasured herbal teas from linden blossoms, thyme, caraway seeds, mint, raspberries, wild strawberries, rosehips, chamomile, dill, etc. They not only refresh and quench your thirst but also cure various ailments.

BAKED GOODS AND SWEET DISHES

Lithuanians have never had much of a sweet tooth. Baked goods and sweet dishes are not a daily food. However, every homemaker tries to pamper her family as inventively as possible during the holidays. Formerly, cakes and other pastries were made at home by families, or using the help of someone known throughout the village for baking.

In the early 20th century, many new foods appeared in our cuisine, including layer cakes and baumkuchens. Some of them became popular and established themselves in Lithuanian cooking. Nowadays, no holiday forgoes the huge baumkuchens that came to us from German cuisine. Many of our most popular baked goods are now commercially produced. They are made according to our own traditional recipes or have come to us from the cuisines of our neighbours. Even now, however, homemade dishes are more highly valued and considered more delicious. Thus, every homemaker tries to have her own distinctive "specialty of the house", with which she entertains esteemed guests and delights her family.

Since ancient times Lithuanians have used the honey of bees for food. They collected the honey of wild bees in forests from the hollows of old trees. Later, they kept beehives on their farmsteads so there would be enough honey for the needs of their families. For many centuries honey served the place of sugar, which was more widely used only in the early 20th century. Even though sugar has become a daily part of our cuisine, it has not succeeded in displacing honey. As a natural and healthy product, honey is a popular sweetener. It is used to enhance the taste of many foods. Honey served to a guest with cheese or milk is a mark of the greatest hospitality.

SEASONINGS

It is difficult to say exactly what seasonings Lithuanian used and when to add flavor to food. Written sources affirm that Lithuanians skillfully seasoned the food they prepared with spices and various herbs. Imported spices that we have known for many centuries include pepper, cloves, cardamon, cinnamon, saffron, ginger, and others that are still used today. Most of them are widely used in canning meat, fish, and vegetables, sausages, desserts, and flavoring various beverages. Spices improve the taste of the dishes being prepared. However, some imported spices are hot and not suitable for our traditional taste. The assortment of imported spices is very limited, too. Most recently, prepared spice mixes have been the main imports used. For this reason, all foods have a similar taste.

Lithuanian homemakers always preferred seasonings grown in their own gardens or gathered in fields, marshes, in or near forests.They used them very moderately and with great skill to enhance the taste of food, enrich it with vitamins, and improve digestion. Many of these seasonings also have healing properties.

The herbs that grow in Lithuania have essential oils and other fragrant substances. They are diverse and provide dishes with a distinctive aroma, stimulate appetite, and improve digestion. In addition, these plants are valued not only as herbs but also as remedies for various ailments and as a rich source of vitamins.

What seasonings should be used in the preparation of food, and in what amounts, – these things depend on the seasonings available, the manner of preparation, and most importantly, one's taste and experience. This is a great art based on experience passed on from generation to generation. Homemakers understood that the seasonings should not overwhelm the taste of the dish but should bring it out. It was said that at the master's table you could no longer taste the fish because it was prepared with all kinds of seasonings. Experienced homemakers knew the unwritten rules, for example, that more than 2–3 kinds of seasonings should not be added to a dish and that they should be added at the end of cooking.

A good homemaker always lays up stores of seasonings. Medicinal herbs and seasonings are dried and put into cloth bags.

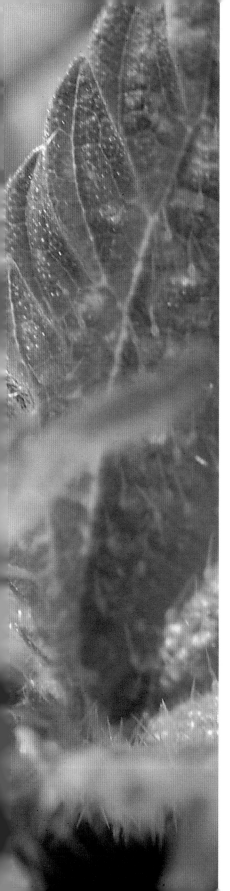

soups

Hemp Soup

Kanapienė

2 raw pickled beets, 1 cup hemp seed, 1 onion, 2 tbsps butter or oil, pepper, salt.

Cut the pickled beets into narrow strips, or grate them on a coarse grater. Add a cup of water, cover, and cook for 15 min.

Brown the hemp seed in a frying pan for 3–5 min. While they are still hot, pour into a mortar, and mash well. Pour the mashed hemp seed into a bowl, add hot boiled water, and strain. Add the strained hemp seed milk to the hot beets, add a finely chopped sautéed onion, ground pepper, and salt. Heat up.

Serve hot with boiled or baked potatoes in their skins.

Hemp Dumpling Soup

Kanapių kukulienė

1 cup boiled and mashed broad beans, 1 cup mashed hemp seed, 2 cloves garlic, pepper, ½ l water, ½ l poppy seed or hemp seed milk.

Brown the hemp seed in a frying pan, mash, and add to the mashed beans. Add finely chopped garlic, pepper, and salt. Knead thoroughly. Make small balls from this mixture, put into boiling salted water, and cook for 10–15 min.

Add poppy seed or hemp seed milk.

Serve hot for dinner.

Blackbird Soup

Švilpokynė

2 cups flour, ½ l milk, 2 eggs, 50 g butter salt, ½ l water.

Beat the eggs while combining with the flour and salt. The result should have the consistency of pancake batter. If necessary, add milk, and beat well.

Pour the water and milk into a pot, and bring to a boil. Into this boiling liquid, spoon elongated pieces of the dough. Cook for 5–10 min.

Add butter to the soup when it is done.

This very popular soup is made for dinner throughout Lithuania. Its other names include leistinė (spooned dumpling soup) and žiurkynė (rat soup).

Pinched Dumpling Soup

Gnaibytinė

2 cups rye or barley flour, ½ l water, ½ l milk or cream.

Knead the flour into a stiff mass with a small amount of water. Pinch off small pieces of dough, and put into boiling salted water. Cook for 10–15 min. Add the milk, cream, or poppy seed or hemp seed milk. Serve for dinner.

Kruopynė

Groat Soup

2 cups any kind of groats (rye, barley, wheat, oats), ½ l water, ½ l milk or cream, 50 g butter, salt.

Soak the groats well, pour into the water, and cook until tender. When they are almost done, add salt, the milk or cream, and butter. Poppy seed or hemp seed milk may also be added. Serve hot, usually for dinner. Formerly, kruopienė (groat soup) was also made for breakfast and eaten as a traditional second mild soup.

Kvietienė

Wheat Soup

200 g wheat, 1 l milk, 1 l water, 2 tbsps sugar, salt.

Wash the wheat well, and soak for 8–10 hrs. After soaking, pour the wheat into a pot, add water and a little salt. Cover the pot, cook over a low flame until the wheat is tender and swollen. After cooking, add the sugar and milk, and bring to a boil.

In Aukštaitija, people made this soup for dinner.

Miltienė

Flour Soup

2 cups rye, barley, or oat flour, ½ l milk or cream, ½ l water, salt.

Stir the flour into salted boiling water, mix constantly to keep lumps from forming. While constantly stirring, cook for 5–10 min. Add the milk or cream. Heat up. Poppy seed or hemp seed milk may also be added to this soup.

Serve hot for dinner.

Duonienė

Bread Soup

300 g black rye bread, 3 potatoes, 100 g butter, 1 onion, 100 g sour cream, salt, ½ l water.

Peel the potatoes, dice into 2-cm cubes, and boil in salted water until tender (10–15 min.). Remove the boiled potatoes, purée through a sieve, and put back into the water in which they were boiled.

In a frying pan, sauté a finely chopped onion in butter and bread sliced into 1-cm cubes.

Add the fried bread to the soup, mix thoroughly, and add sour cream.

Serve bread soup for in dinner.

Duonsriubė

Bread Soup

½ kg potatoes, 1 cup rye flour, 1 l milk, salt.

Peel and dice the potatoes, put into a pot, add salt and water, and bring to a boil. Add small dumplings made from the flour. Cook for 10–15 min. Add the milk, and heat up.

This soup is a dinner time favorite in Suvalkija.

Nettle Soup

Dilgėlynė

*300 g young nettle, leaves,
2 onions, 2 carrots, 1 tbsp flour,
50 g butter, 200 g sour cream,
salt, 1 l water.*

Slice the carrots, add water, and cook in a pot until tender.

Wash the nettle leaves, put into a separate pot of boiling salted water (about ½ l), and boil for 1–2 minutes. Empty the boiled leaves into a colander, and chop finely. Heat the butter in a frying pan, add finely chopped onions and flour, sauté for 5 minutes, add the chopped nettles, and stew for 3–5 min. after adding a little of the liquid from the boiled carrots. Add the stewed nettles to the strained carrot broth, cook for 1–2 min., add salt.

Add sour cream to the soup after it is done.

Nettle soup is served hot with boiled or baked potatoes or black bread.

This seasonal soup is most popular in early spring, when the first shoots have just appeared.

Sorrel Soup

Rūgštėlynė

*6 potatoes, ½ cup barley groats,
200 g sorrel, 1 hard-boiled egg,
200 g sour cream, salt, ½ l water.*

Peel, wash, and dice the potatoes, put into a pot, add water and the groats after soaking, bring to a boil. When the potatoes and groats are almost done, add the washed and chopped sorrel and salt. Cook for 10–15 min.

Before eating, add a chopped egg and sour cream.

Serve hot with hot potatoes or bread.

Sour Leaf Soup

Rūgšti lapienė

*300 g young beet leaves, 200 g sorrel,
200 g sour cream, salt, 1 l water.*

Chop the beet leaves and sorrel, and cook in salted water. Add sour cream, and heat up, but do not boil. Serve with hot potatoes or black bread.

Sorrel Soup with Mushrooms

Rūgštynių sriuba su grybais

*1 onion, 1 carrot, 1 bunch parsley,
4–5 dried mushrooms, 2 egg yolks,
½ cup sour cream, 200 g sorrel, salt.*

Pour cold water over the dried mushrooms, and soak for 2–3 hrs. Pour them into a pot with all of the liquid in which they were soaked. Chop the potherbs, add them and 1 l water, and cook until the vegetables are tender. Strain the broth. Thinly slice the cooked mushrooms, chop the sorrel leaves, and add both to the broth. Add salt, and cook for 5–10 min. Add the sour cream and hard-boiled egg yolks (half a hard-boiled egg may also be added to each bowl of soup). Eat hot with boiled or baked potatoes.

Mushroom Soup

Grybienė

½ l salted or fresh mushrooms,
5 potatoes (medium-sized),
100 g butter, 2 onions, 2 carrots,
2 cloves garlic, 4–5 dill sprigs,
5 peppercorns, 100 g butter,
200 g sour cream, 1½ l water, salt.

If the mushrooms are fresh, clean, slice, and wash well, changing the water several times. If salted mushrooms are used, soak well, and wash.

Finely chop the onions, and sauté in butter.

Add to a pot of water the prepared mushrooms, thinly sliced carrots, diced potatoes, seasonings, sautéed onions, and salt. Cook over a low flame until the carrots and potatoes are tender (about 20–25 min.). Then add the remaining butter, heat up again, add sour cream, and bring to a boil.

Serve hot with bread.

Potato Soup with Dried Mushrooms

Bulbynė su džiovintais grybais

6 potatoes, 4–5 dried king bolete
mushrooms, 2 tbsps barley groats,
50 g butter, 100 g sour cream,
2 bay leaves, 2–3 dill sprigs,
4 peppercorns, 1½ l water, salt.

Wash the king bolete mushrooms well, and soak for 2–3 hrs. Separately soak the barley groats for the same length of time. Thinly slice the soaked mushrooms, put into a pot, and add the water in which they were soaked as well as the remaining water. Cook over a low flame. When the mushrooms come to a boil, add the soaked groats. Cook for 15–20 min., then add the potatoes after peeling and dicing, the seasonings, butter, and salt, and continue cooking until the potatoes are tender.

When the soup is done, add sour cream.

Serve hot with black bread.

Potato Soup

Bulvienė

6 potatoes, 3 carrots,
1 l milk, 50 g butter,
½ l water, dill, salt.

Peel the potatoes, and cut into strips, cook briefly in a small amount of salted water. Add coarsely grated carrots, and cook until tender. Then add chopped dill and milk, and heat to boiling, add butter.

Serve for dinner.

Sour Potato Soup

Rūgšti bulvienė

6 potatoes, 3 tbsps flour or
soaked barley, groats,
½ l buttermilk, 1 cup sour
cream, 50 g butter, tarragon,
½ l water, salt.

Peel and dice the potatoes, put into salted boiling water, and cook over a low flame. When the potatoes are tender, slowly, while constantly stirring, add the flour or groats and the tarragon. Cook for 5 min. While carefully stirring, add the buttermilk, add the sour cream and butter, and heat up, but do not bring to a boil.

Serve with bread.

Potato Dumpling Soup

Bulvių kukulienė

1 kg raw potatoes,
3 boiled potatoes,
1 l milk, 1 l water,
tarragon.

Peel the raw potatoes, grate finely, and squeeze out. Leave the liquid from the squeezed potatoes in the bowl for 5–10 min. for the starch to settle. Then pour off the liquid, add the starch to the squeezed potatoes, add the boiled potatoes after mashing, add salt, crushed tarragon, and knead. Make dumplings 1–2 cm in diameter, and put into boiling salted water. Cook for 10–15 min.

After cooking, add the milk, and bring to a boil.

Sometimes poppy seed or hemp seed milk is also added.

Half-Dumpling Soup

Pusinė "zacirka"

4 potatoes, 1 cup flour,
1 l milk or cream, 20 g butter,
½ l water, tarragon, salt.

Peel and grate the potatoes, mix with the wheat flour, add crushed tarragon and salt, mix, and spoon into boiling salted water. Cook for 10–15 min. After cooking, add the milk or cream, heat up, add butter.

Potato Soup with Poppy Seeds and Milk

Bulvienė su aguonomis ir pienu

5 potatoes, 1 cup poppy seeds,
100 g sugar, 50 g butter,
1 l water, salt.

Pour boiling water over the poppy seeds, and soak for 2–3 hrs. so that they swell up. After pouring off the water, run the poppy seeds through a meat grinder 2–3 times, or mash well. Add 1 l boiled cold water to the ground poppy seeds, mix well, and strain through a sieve. Add sugar to the resulting poppy seed milk, and mix. Peel and dice the potatoes, and put into a small amount (½ l) of boiling salted water. Cook over a low flame. When the potatoes start getting soggy, slowly, while constantly stirring, add the poppy seed milk and butter, and while continuing to stir, heat up again, but do not bring to a boil. Serve potato soup with black bread for dinner.

Potato Soup

Bulvių putra

10 potatoes, 1 l milk,
50 g butter, dill,
½ l water, salt.

Peel the potatoes, cut into pieces, and cook in salted water. Drain the tender potatoes, but save the liquid. Mash the drained potatoes, add some of the liquid in which they were boiled, and mix well. Then add the sweet milk, bring to a boil, add butter and finely chopped dill. Serve this soup with bread and butter.

Grated Potato Soup

Tarkynė

4 potatoes, 1 cup sweet cream, tarragon, salt, 1 l water.

Peel the potatoes, and grate finely. Bring the water to a boil, and while constantly stirring with a spatula or spoon, add the grated potatoes and tarragon. While constantly stirring, cook over a low flame (about 10 min.) until tender. After cooking, add the salt and cream. Mix well.

Serve for dinner.

Instead of cream, poppy seed or hemp seed milk may also be used.

Vegetable Soup

Daržovienė

1 small rutabaga, 2 carrots, 1 cup green peas, ½ small head of cabbage, several dill sprigs, 1 l water, 1 l sweet milk, salt.

Dice the rutabaga into small cubes, chop the cabbage, finely slice or coarsely grate the carrots, add the peas, water, and salt, and cook until tender (10–15 min.). After cooking, add the milk and chopped dill, heat to boiling. Vegetable soup is made in various ways, with substitutes for one vegetable or another.

It is especially popular in summer and early fall.

Sauerkraut Soup with Mushrooms

Kopūstienė su grybais

200 g fresh, pickled, or salted, mushrooms, ½ l sauerkraut, 1 carrot, 1 onion, 4 peppercorns, 2 bay leaves, 200 g sour cream, salt, 2 l water.

Clean and wash the mushrooms if they are fresh, soak well and wash if they are salted or pickled. Put into a pot, add water, and cook. After removing the foam, add the sauerkraut and a whole onion, which should be removed when somewhat tender so that it does not become soggy. Cook for about 20 min. When the soup is almost done, add the peppercorns, the bay leaves, a coarsely grated carrot, and salt, cook for 10 min. Add sour cream. Mix thoroughly. Sauerkraut soup with mushrooms is often made in late autumn and winter.

Serve hot with boiled potatoes or bread.

Hot sauerkraut soup is often eaten with cold potatoes boiled in their skins.

Rutabaga Soup

Griežtienė

1 rutabaga (medium-sized), 3 potatoes, 1 l milk or cream, 1 carrot, dill, ½ l water.

Pour the water into a pot, add the rutabaga and potatoes after dicing, cook until tender. Then add a finely grated carrot and dill, cook for 2–3 min. After cooking, add the milk or cream and salt. Usually eaten for dinner.

Turnip Soup

Gručkienė

½ kg potatoes, 200 g turnips, 1 l milk, 50 g butter, dill, salt.

Peel and dice the potatoes, thinly slice the turnips, add water, salt, and a stem of dill, and cook until tender. Add the milk to the cooked turnip soup, heat to boiling, add butter and finely chopped dill sprigs.

Serve hot for dinner.

Onion Soup

"Cibulynė"

1 herring, 2–3 onions, 3 peeled boiled potatoes, ½ l boiled water, ½ l beet brine, 5 peppercorns, salt.

Clean, wash, and drain the herring, wrap in paper, and bake on charcoal embers for 10–15 min. Unwrap the baked herring from the paper, and remove the bones. Mash the pieces of herring in a clay bowl with a wooden spoon together with the peeled potatoes. Pour cold boiled water on this mashed mixture, mix well, add thinly sliced onions and finely ground peppercorns, add beet brine and, if necessary, salt. Mix everything thoroughly.

Serve onion soup with hot boiled potatoes in their skins.

This onion soup is popular in Žemaitija.

Potato Soup with Fish

Žuvų bulvienė

7–8 dried or salted small fish, 5–6 potatoes, 3 tbsps barley groats, 50 g butter, 100 g sour cream, tarragon, dill, pepper, 1½ l water.

Soak the dried or salted fish for 20–25 min. in cold water, wash, put into a pot, add cold water and soaked groats, heat up. When the water comes to a boil, add peeled and thinly sliced potatoes. Cook for 15–20 min., until the potatoes are tender. Then add butter and sour cream. Heat up, but do not bring to a boil. Add salt if needed.

Serve with bread for lunch or dinner.

Fish Soup

Žuvienė

1 kg fish, 3–4 potatoes, 1 onion, 1 carrot, 3 black peppercorns, 4 allspice berries, 3 bay leaves, 1 stem fresh or dried dill, 20 g butter, 2 l water.

Clean the fish, remove the gills, wash, put into cold water, add a chopped onion, a sliced carrot, a stem of dill, the pepper, allspice, and bay leaves, and cook over a low flame for about an hour. Remove the cooked fish, strain the broth, add diced potatoes and salt, and cook for 10–15 min. After cooking, add pieces of boned fish, butter, and finely chopped dill.

Soup from various kinds of fish is most often made by fishermen and people who live near the Baltic Sea and the Curonian Lagoon.

Herring Soup

Silkynė

2 herrings, 2 onions, 2 pickled beets, 200 g sour cream, 7–8 peppercorns, salt, 1 l water.

Slice the beets into narrow strips, put into a pot of cold water, add thinly sliced onions and peppercorns. Heat and cook for 10–15 min. Peel the herring, remove their bones, partially fry the fillets in a pan. Slice the fried herring fillets into little pieces, add to the cooked beets, and bring to a boil. Add sour cream.

Serve herring soup hot with boiled or baked potatoes.

Carp Soup

Karpienė

½ kg carp, 1 parsley root, 1 leek, 1 onion, 1 small piece celery, parsley, celery leaves, 3 tbsps flour, 2 eggs, 100 g cooking oil, salt, 1 l water.

Scale and clean the carp, remove the gills, cut off the head, peel, and remove the bones. Cut the carp fillet into small pieces, roll in flour, and fry in heated oil. Pour water into a pot, add all of the carp pieces (the bones, head, skin) and chopped potherbs, cook over a low flame for about 30 min. Strain the cooked broth, add the fried pieces of fish and salt, heat up. After cooking, add beaten egg yolks.

Before eating, add finely chopped parsley and celery leaves.

Serve hot with bread.

Fish Dumpling Soup

Žuvų kukulienė

½ kg fresh fish, 2 onions, 1 egg, 20 g butter, 3 tbsps dried bread crumbs, 2 tbsps sour cream, 3–4 peppercorns, 1 lovage sprig, 1 carrot, 1 parsley root with leaves, 1 leek, salt, 1 l water.

Clean and peel the fish, remove the bones, grind, add finely chopped onions sautéed in butter, add sour cream, dried bread crumbs, ground pepper, crushed lovage leaves, and salt. Mix thoroughly to make a fluffy and homogeneous mixture. Pour water into a pot, add all of the fish remnants (the bones, head, skin, and fins), chopped potherbs (the carrot, parsley root, leek, and sprig of lovage), and salt, cook for 25–30 min. Strain the resulting broth, pour back into the pot, and again bring to a boil. To this boiling vegetable broth add small (walnut-sized) dumplings made from this fish mixture. Cook for 15–20 min. After cooking, add chopped parsley leaves to the soup.

Serve hot. Some people like to add sour cream.

Mixed Vegetable Soup

Šiupinynė

½ cup peas, ½ cup broad beans, 3 potatoes, 1 carrot, parsley, dill, 100 g butter, 100 g sour cream, 1½ l water, salt.

After soaking, pour the beans and peas into a pot of cold water, and cook until almost tender. Add a coarsely grated carrot, thinly sliced potatoes, butter, seasoning, and salt. Cover tightly, cook until the vegetables are tender. Use only large sprigs of parsley and dill so that they can be removed after cooking.

After the soup is done, add sour cream and chopped sprigs of fresh parsley and dill. Serve with bread.

Garden Bean Soup

Pupelynė

1 cup garden beans, 1 carrot, 3 potatoes, 1 l milk or cream, parsley, dill, salt.

Soak the beans, put them into a pot. Dice the potatoes, add to the beans along with the carrot, salt, and enough water to cover everything. Cook until the vegetables are tender. After cooking, add the milk or cream, add chopped dill and parsley, heat to boiling.

Poppy seed milk may also be added to this soup. Serve for dinner.

Broad Bean Soup

Pupienė

½ l broad beans, 2 potatoes, 1 carrot, ½ l sour cream, 1 tsp sage, salt, water.

Add ½ l of water to the soaked beans, and cook until tender. Peel the potatoes and carrot, dice finely, and add to the boiling beans, add salt and sage, and finish cooking.

Before eating, add the sour cream, and mix. Serve hot with bread.

Beet Soup with Mushrooms

Burokienė su grybais

2 boiled pickled beets, 1 carrot, 1 onion, 5-6 dried mushrooms, 5 peppercorns, 2 bay leaves, 1½ l water, salt, 4 tbsps sour cream or cooking oil, ½ cup pickled-beet brine.

Wash the dried mushrooms, add to cold water, and soak for 2-3 hrs. Then cook for 15-20 min. in the same water. Remove, slice, and continue cooking. Add a thinly sliced carrot, the onion, and the seasonings. Cook for 20 min. over a low flame. Then remove the onion from the broth, add coarsely grated beets, the beet brine, and salt. Mix thoroughly, and heat up. Before serving, add sour cream. Eat with hot potatoes or black bread. Beet soup with mushrooms is a traditional food on Christmas Eve. In Žemaitija, people like beet soup cooked with poppy seed or hemp seed milk.

In Dzūkija, people call this soup mushroom brine (grybų rasalas). They cook a grated beet with mushrooms and add barley groats.

Beet Broth with Little Ear Dumplings

Baršteliai su ausytėmis

3 boiled pickled beets,
150 g potherbs (1 onion, parsley, dill,
celery, carrot), 5 peppercorns,
1 bay leaf, 1 tsp starch,
2-3 slices dried bread,
5-6 dried mushrooms, 2 l water.
FOR THE LITTLE EAR DUMPLINGS:
1 cup flour, ½ egg, water.
FOR THE FILLING:
100 g boiled dried mushrooms
(boiled in broth), ½ onion,
20 g butter, ½ egg, oregano,
marjoram, salt.

Cook a broth from the herbs, seasonings, and dried mushrooms (after soaking 3 hrs.). Remove the mushrooms when tender, strain the broth, and pour over coarsely grated beets and dried bread slices. Keep covered for about 30 min., and strain again. Add dissolved starch to the broth, heat to boiling, but do not boil. Add salt.

To make the little ear dumplings of flour, egg, water, and salt, knead the dough to medium stiffness, roll thinly, and cut into 3-cm squares.

Mash the mushrooms cooked in the broth, add a finely chopped onion sautéed in butter, add salt, oregano, and marjoram, and heat the mixture in a frying pan with butter. Add a beaten egg, mix well, and put little balls of the resulting mixture on the squares of dough. Apply egg white to their edges, fold like a triangular scarf, squeeze the edges and corners together to make them into little ears. Put these little ears into boiling, slightly salted water. Boil for 5-10 min. (until they rise to the surface). After boiling, remove them, put into warmed bowls, and add the hot beet broth.

Beet broth with little ear dumplings is made for dinner on Christmas Eve.

Beet Soup with Mushrooms and Herring

Barščiai su grybais ir silke

200 g salted or pickled mushrooms,
3-4 pickled beets, 1 herring,
1 onion, 5-6 peppercorns,
4 bay leaves, 3 potatoes,
100 g sour cream or cooking oil,
2 l water, salt.

Soak the mushrooms well, wash, put into cold water, and heat up. Before they come to a boil, remove the foam. Once they are boiling, add coarsely grated beets, finely diced potatoes, and seasonings. Add a whole onion, which will be removed when the soup is almost done. Cook everything for 20-25 min. Peel the herring, remove the bones, slice into small pieces, and add to the soup when it is almost done. Cook for 5 more min.

Before serving, add sour cream and, if necessary, salt.

Serve this soup with hot potatoes.

Beet Stalk Soup

Lambai

200 g beet leaves with their stalks,
½ l water, ½ l sour milk, 100 g sour
cream, 2-3 small cucumbers,
50 g green onions, dill sprigs, salt.

Thoroughly wash the beet leaves with their stalks, chop, and cook in water. Let cool. In a bowl, combine thinly sliced cucumbers, chopped dill, and sliced green onions, add sour milk, sour cream, and salt, mix well, and add the cooked beets with all of their liquid. Mix thoroughly. Add salt if needed. Serve with hot potatoes.

This is a summer time soup made on hot days.

Cold Beet Soup

Šaltibarščiai

*2 cooked red beets, 2 cucumbers,
2 hard-boiled eggs, 100 g sour
cream, 1 l sour milk, 1 cup boiled
water, 8–10 dill sprigs, 100 g green
onions, ½ tsp salt.*

Mix the egg yolks with finely chopped green onions and salt. Add finely diced cucumbers, diced egg whites, coarsely grated beets, sour cream, sour milk, and cold boiled water, mix well. Pour into bowls, and add finely chopped dill. Do not mix.

Serve with hot potatoes.

This soup is most popular on hot summer days.

Aukštaičių Cold Sorrel Soup

Aukštaitiški šaltibarščiai

*400 g sorrel, 200 g cream,
3 cucumbers, 2 hard-boiled eggs,
10–15 dill sprigs, 100 g green
onions, 1 l water, salt.*

Chop the sorrel, add to boiling water, and cook for 5–10 min., then let cool, and refrigerate. In a separate pot, add a little of the sorrel broth, thoroughly mix with the cream, and pour over the cooked sorrel. Add finely diced cucumbers, finely chopped green onions, dill sprigs, diced eggs, and salt. Mix well.

Serve with hot boiled potatoes on hot summer days.

Cold Beet Soup with Tree Sap

Medžių sulos šaltibarščiai

*1 l birch or maple sap, 2 boiled pickled
beets, 1 cucumber or borage leaves,
1 hard-boiled egg, 100 g sour cream,
green onions, dill sprigs, salt.*

Pour the sap into a bowl, add beets cut into thin strips, finely diced cucumbers or chopped borage leaves, chopped egg, finely chopped green onions, dill sprigs, sour cream, and salt. Mix well.

Serve with hot boiled or baked potatoes.

Bread and Berry Soup

Mutinys

*200 g black rye bread,
3 tbsps honey or sugar, 1 cup
mashed berries (any kind), 1 l water.*

Dissolve the honey or sugar in 1 liter of cold boiled water, add the berries, add the bread after dicing into 1–2 cm cubes. Mix well.

This is a summer afternoon food. Homemakers used to bring this soup to family members working in the fields.

Bread and berry soup is very popular throughout Lithuania. Its colour and acidity depend on the kind of berries used.

Bread and Sap Soup

Mutinys su sula

1 l birch sap, 200 g black rye bread, 2–3 tbsps honey or sugar.

Dice the bread, add to the fresh or fermented birch sap, and sweeten.
Eat on hot days in the afternoon or morning.

Bread Soup with Hazelnuts

Mekeris

200 g black bread, ½ cup finely chopped hazelnuts, 2 tbsps sour cream, 2 tbsps sugar, ½ l cold boiled water.

Pour the cold boiled water over finely diced bread, and let stand for 2–3 hrs. Then add the sugar and finely chopped hazelnuts, mix well.

Serve cold. Add sour cream.

Bread soup with hazelnuts has a sweet and sour flavor.

For this reason, it is very popular on hot summer days.

Cold Soup

Šaltsriubė

½ l berries, ½ cup sugar, 2 tbsps starch, 4 tbsps sour cream, 1 cinnamon stick, 1 l water.

Dissolve the starch in a cup of cold water. Pour the remaining water into a pot, add the sugar and cinnamon, bring to a boil. Add the berries to this boiling syrup. When it again comes to a boil, add the starchy water. Again bring to a boil, let cool, and refrigerate. Pour into bowls, add sour cream. Do not mix. By using different berries or fruit, it is possible to make a different cold soup every day.

Cherry Soup

Vyšnainė

½ l cherries, 200 g bread, 3–4 tbsps sugar or honey, 1 l milk.

Pit and mash the cherries, dice the bread, add the milk and honey or sugar. Mix well.

Serve in the afternoon or for dinner.

By using different kinds of berries, we can have avietienė (raspberry soup), žemuogienė (wild strawberry soup), serbentienė (currant soup), mėlynienė (blueberry soup).

Poppy seed Soup

Aguonienė

1 cup poppy seeds, ½ l boiled water, 2 cups diced dried black bread, 2–3 tbsps honey.

Pour boiling water over the poppy seeds, let stand for 2–3 hrs., drain, and grind twice. Pour cold boiled water over the ground poppy seeds, add the honey and diced bread, mix well.

Serve for dinner.

This soup is especially suitable on warm summer days.

grains

Black Rye Bread

Juoda ruginė duona

3 kg coarsely ground sifted rye flour, 1 l water, leftover dough from last time's baking, salt.
FOR THE DOUGH:
½ kg rye flour, 50 g yeast, 1 l warm water.

For black rye bread to rise, a 1-kg lump of unused dough from the last baking is used. Keep it in a large bowl in a dry, cool place (at a temperature no lower than 0 °C) until the next baking. Before baking the new bread, dissolve the dough in warm water, and pour into the dough being mixed.

If there is no leftover dough, some must be made before baking. To do so, mix all the ingredients in the recipe thoroughly, and keep warm so they ferment. After 24 hours, the leftover dough will be ready to use. Leftover dough gives bread a pleasant sour taste. Each piece of leftover dough has a different taste. Sometimes a cup of sour milk is added for a different taste.

Warm the water for the bread to 40–45 °C, add a third of the flour as well as the leftover dough. After mixing well, sprinkle flour on the surface of the dough. Cover the large bowl warmly, and put in a warm place so the dough can ferment. During fermentation, it will get 2–3 times bigger, so after mixing and placing it in a large bowl, the mixture should fill no more that one fourth of the bowl. After the dough is sufficiently fermented, after about 14 hrs., beat well, and after adding the remaining flour as well as salt. Knead very well. Flatten the surface of the dough, and moisten with a wet hand, cover the dough warmly, and keep in a warm place until it rises (for 2–3 hrs.).

Line the baking pans with dried maple, cabbage, sweet-flag leaves or with sprinkled flour. Make oblong loaves by flattening the surface of the bread with a damp hand and pressing in the sides with one's fingers. Bake in a hot oven (220 °C) for 2–3 hrs. If the bottom of the loaf sounds hollow when tapped with one's fingers, the bread is done.

After removing from the oven, moisten the surface of the loaves with cold water. Cover with a cloth and let cool. Warm loaves may not be put in a cold room, placed on top of each other or squeezed.

If kept in a cool place, bread will stay fresh for 1–2 weeks.

Hot Water Rye Bread

Plikyta ruginė duona

2 kg rye flour, 1½ l water, ½ cup caraway seeds, salt, leavening, dried cabbage, sweet-flag, or maple leaves as lining.

Pour boiling water over a third of the rye flour, and mix well so that no dry flour remains. Cover the kneading trough warmly, leave for 4–5 hrs. so that the mixture cools off. Then add the leftover dough that has been dissolved in warm water, and beat well. Again cover the kneading trough warmly, and keep in a warm place for about 24 hrs. (sometimes the dough ferments for up to 2–3 days). Beat the fermenting mixture some 4–5 times to aerate the dough.

Once fermentation is complete, add the remaining flour, the caraway seeds, the salt, and knead for a long time until the dough no longer sticks to your hands. Then after again covering it and putting it in a warm place, let it rise for at least 5–6 hrs. (hot water bread takes longer to rise).

After the dough has risen, with hands dampened with water, make one large or two small loaves, put into a baking pan lined with cabbage, sweet-flag, or maple leaves (if they are not available, sprinkle flour in the pan), and bake in a hot oven for about 2 hrs. until the bread becomes lighter. After removing, moisten with water, cover with a cloth, and let cool.

Hot water bread has a sweet and sour taste and does not get stale for a long time.

Black Rye Potato Bread

uoda ruginė duona su bulvėmis

10 kg rye flour, 4 l water, 2 kg potatoes, 100 g salt, leavening.

Boil the potatoes in their skins, peel, and mash or grind with a meat grinder. Mix a third of the rye flour, the leavening (after dissolving in warm water), and the potatoes with water warmed to 35 °C. After mixing thoroughly, sprinkle flour on the dough, and put in a warm place to ferment. Further prepare the dough as for ordinary bread. When baked with potatoes, bread is fluffier and softer.

Yeast Bread

Duona su mielėmis

3 l rye flour, 3 tbsps sugar, 50 g yeast, 1 l whey (or sour milk or water), ½ cup caraway seeds, salt, ½ cup beer or water for moistening.

Warm the whey to a temperature of 30–35 °C, add yeast combined with sugar, and let rise for 15–20 min. After the whey has risen, add half the flour and mix well. Again cover warmly, and let rise for about an hour. To the risen dough, add all the remaining flour, the caraway seeds, and salt, and knead until the dough no longer sticks to your hands. After again covering, let rise well in a warm place for 1½ hrs. From this risen dough, with wet hands, make two small oblong loaves. Put these loaves into a baking pan lined with maple, sweet-flag, or cabbage leaves or sprinkled with flour, and put in a warm place to continue rising. Moisten the tops of the risen loaves with beer or water.

Bake the bread in a hot oven for about 2 hrs. After removing, moisten the loaves with water, and cover with a linen napkin until they cool off to make their crust soft.

Baked Garlic Bread

Pakepinta duona su česnaku

200 g black rye bread, 20 g garlic, 50 g cooking oil, salt.

Cut the bread into slices 1 cm thick. Cut the crusts off the bread slices. Cut the slices into smaller pieces. Fry the pieces of bread on both sides in cooking oil until they turn golden brown.

After removing from the oil, rub garlic into the bread, and sprinkle with salt. Eat with other dishes, or serve with beer.

Rye Porridge

Ruginė košė

*1 cup rye flour, 2 cups water,
100 g butter, salt.*

While constantly stirring, gradually add the rye flour to salted boiling water.
Cook over a low flame, constantly stirring for about 10 min. Then add the
butter, and while stirring, heat for 2–3 more min.

Serve with milk or buttermilk sauce (add chopped onion to the buttermilk).

Rye Porridge with Grated Potatoes

Ruginė košė su bulvių tarkiais

*1 cup rye flour, 1 cup grated
potatoes, 3 cups water, salt.*

Pour the flour in a thin stream into boiling water, and stir so that it does not
form lumps. While constantly stirring, heat, add the grated potatoes and salt.
While stirring, cook for 10 min.

Serve hot with sweet or sour milk.

Rye Porridge with Herring

Ruginė košė su silkėmis

*3 cups rye flour, 3 herring,
¼ tsp coriander,
4 cups water, salt.*

Bring the water to a boil in a pot, and gradually, while constantly stirring, add
the flour, a little salt, and crushed coriander, and while constantly stirring,
cook for 10 min.

After cooking, spoon the porridge into a bowl to form a small heap. Into
this porridge stick the herring (cleaned, peeled, and cut into halves) in such a
way that the ends of their heads and tails stick out. In this way, the herring
are cooked, become tender, and release their saltiness and fat.

Rye Porridge with Apples

Ruginė košė su obuoliais

*2 cups rye flour, 3 cups water,
3 apples, salt, sugar.*

Peel the apples, cut into thin slices, put into a pot, add water, and bring to a
boil. Into these boiling apples, pour the flour in a thin stream while constantly
stirring to keep lumps from forming. Add sugar to the boiling porridge. Cook
for 10 min. while constantly stirring. Serve with milk.

Naturally Leavened Dumplings

Pakilučiai

*3 cups rye flour, 1 cup whey,
100 g butter, 100 g sour
cream, salt.*

Knead the flour with the whey. Add salt. Prepare a somewhat stiff dough, and
after covering, set in a warm place to rise.

From this dough make dumplings, and cook in a pot over steam (after in-
serting a steamer basket) until they puff up nicely (for about 5–10 min.).

Serve hot with melted butter and sour cream.

Bread Dumplings

Duonkukuliai

*3 cups rye flour, 100 g butter,
1 cup sour cream, 1 onion,
2 tbsps caraway seeds,
dill sprigs, green
onions or chives.*

Prepare a somewhat stiff dough from the flour, caraway seeds, and a small amount of water.

From this dough make walnut-sized dumplings, and put into salted boiling water. Cook for 15–20 min.

To make the sauce, finely chop the onion, and sauté in a teaspoon of butter. When the onion is almost done, add the remaining butter, the sour cream, and salt, mix well, and bring to a boil.

Remove the cooked dumplings from the water with a slotted ladle, drain, put into a bowl, and add the sauce. Sprinkle with chopped dill, green onions.

Bread Dumplings with Cottage Cheese

Duonkukuliai su varške

*2 cups rye flour, 200 g cottage cheese,
2 eggs, ½ tsp tarragon, mint leaves,
100 g butter, 100 g sour cream, salt.*

Mash the cottage cheese well, add the flour, eggs, crushed tarragon, and salt, and knead everything. From this dough make little dumplings, and put into salted boiling water. Cook until they rise to the surface of the water (for about 5–8 min.).

Remove the cooked dumplings with a slotted ladle, drain, put into a bowl, add melted butter and sour cream, and sprinkle with chopped mint.

Naturally Leavened Bread Rolls

Parūgėliai

*3 cups rye flour, 2 cups water,
2 tbsps caraway seeds, salt.
FOR THE SAUCE:
200 g cottage cheese,
200 g sour cream.*

In the evening, mix one cup of flour with water, add the caraway seeds, cover, set in a warm place, and let ferment overnight. The next morning, add the remaining flour and the salt, and beat into a dough thicker than pancake batter.

Bake the bread rolls in a well-heated, greased baking pan. Into this baking pan, spoon the bread rolls, and bake in a slow to moderate oven (180 °C) until they rise, puff up, and turn golden brown.

Serve hot with cottage cheese sauce. For the sauce, mash the cottage cheese, and mix with the sour cream.

Rye Pancakes

Ruginiai blynai

*2 cups rye flour, ½ cup whey or sour
milk, 2 eggs, 200 g cottage cheese,
100 g sour cream, cooking fat, salt.*

Pour the whey or sour milk into a bowl, add the eggs, flour, and salt. Whip into a somewhat thick batter.

Spoon the batter into the heated fat in a frying pan, and fry the pan-cakes on both sides until they are golden brown.

Serve with mashed cottage cheese and sour cream.

Kvietinė košė

½ l wheat flour,
1 l milk, salt, 50 g butter.

Wheat Porridge

While constantly stirring, pour the flour in boiling milk a little bit at a time, and add salt. Cook for 5–10 min. while constantly stirring over a low flame. After cooking, spoon the porridge into a bowl, make a small indentation in the middle of the porridge, and add the butter.

Serve with sweet milk.

Virtiniai

3 cups wheat flour,
1 egg, 1 cup water, salt.

Dumplings

Knead the flour, egg, and salted water very well into a stiff dough. Roll the dough to a thickness of 2 mm, press out little circles (5 cm in diameter), put 1 teaspoon of filling in the middle of them, fold in half, and squeeze the sides together. Put the dumplings into boiling salted water, and cook for 10–15 min.

Dumplings are a popular food in the Aukštaitija region. They are usually made for breakfast. Serve with butter and sour cream sauce.

Dumplings are made with various fillings throughout Lithuania.

Virtų bulvių įdaras

300 g boiled potatoes, 50 g butter,
1 onion, 1 egg, 1 tsp oregano, salt.

Boiled Potato Filling

Mash the boiled potatoes. Add a finely chopped onion sautéed in butter, add crushed oregano, an egg, salt, mix well.

Grybų įdaras

50 g dried mushrooms, 2 onions,
50 g butter, 1 tsp lemon balm,
1 tbsp bread crumbs, salt.

Mushroom Filling

Soak the mushrooms for 2–3 hrs. Boil the soaked mushrooms in the same water in which they were soaked. Finely chop the boiled mushrooms. Finely chop the onions, and sauté in butter, add the mushrooms, chopped lemon balm, bread crumbs, salt, and sauté every-thing for another 3–5 min.

Serve these dumplings with a sauce made from the mushroom broth mixed with sour cream.

Varškės įdaras

300 g cottage cheese,
1 egg, 1 tbsp mint, salt.

Cottage Cheese Filling

Mash the cottage cheese well with the egg, add chopped mint and salt, and mix well.

You can serve cottage cheese dumplings with a sauce made from melted butter and sour cream.

In the Žemaitija region, people eat these dumplings with sour cream to which they have added chopped southernwood leaves.

Berry and Fruit Filling

Uogų ir vaisių įdaras

300 g berries (blueberries or pitted cherries) or apples, ½ tbsp cinnamon, ½ cup sugar.

Mix the cherries, blueberries, or other berries with the sugar, and add 1 teaspoon to each dumpling. Peel the apples, slice finely, and stew for 5–10 min. with the sugar and cinnamon. After cooling, add 1 teaspoon to each dumpling.

Poppy Seed Filling

Aguonų įdaras

1 cup poppy seeds, 100 g sugar, 1 tsp lemon balm.

Wash the poppy seeds, add hot water, and let swell for 2 hrs. Drain the seeds, and grind 2–3 times with a meat grinder. Add chopped lemon balm and sugar to the ground poppy seeds, and mix well. Add 1 teaspoon of these poppy seeds to each dumpling.

Serve these dumplings hot or cold with sour cream and sugar.

Hemp Seed Filling

Kanapių įdaras

1 cup hemp seed, 20 g butter, 1 onion, 1 egg, 1 tbsp bread crumbs, salt.

Soak the hemp seed and boil for 10-15 min. Drain the boiled hemp seed, grind with a meat grinder, or mash. Finely chop the onion, sauté in butter, and add to the ground hemp seed. Add the egg, bread crumbs, and salt, mix thoroughly.

Hemp Seed and Mushroom Filling

Kanapių ir grybų įdaras

1 cup hemp seed, 1 cup boiled and ground dried mushrooms, 1 onion, 25 g butter, 1 egg, 1 tbsp marjoram, pepper, salt.

Fry the hemp seed in a frying pan, and grind twice with a meat grinder. Add the ground mushrooms, ground onion, chopped marjoram, ground pepper, butter, egg, and salt, and fry everything in the frying pan.

Serve these dumplings with melted butter or sour cream.

Yeast Pancakes

Mieliniai blynai

2 cups flour, 50 g yeast, 2 eggs, 2 cups milk, 2 tbsps sugar, cooking fat, 100 g sour cream, 3 tbsps sugar or berry preserves (of any kind), salt.

Warm the milk to 35-40 °C, add yeast combined with sugar and 2 tbsps of flour, and mix well. Sprinkle flour on top, and leave in a warm place for 30 min. to rise.

Separate the egg yolks from the whites, and beat the yolks with salt.

To the risen batter, add the remaining flour and beaten egg yolks, mix well, and put in a warm place to rise for I hour. Add the beaten egg whites to the risen batter, fold in, and fry the pancakes in heated fat over a low flame.

Serve hot with sour cream and sugar, berry preserves or apple sauce.

Yeast pancakes are a traditional food on Shrove Tuesday. They are served to visitors who are in costume.

Prune Pancakes

Blyneliai su slyvomis

*300 g prunes, 2 eggs,
2 cups flour, ½ cup sour cream,
2 tbsps powdered sugar,
salt, water, cooking fat.*

Soak the prunes well in warm water, wash, and cut them in half.

To the flour, add the eggs, sour cream, salt, and a little water, and beat well. If the batter is too thick (it should fall easily from the spoon), add more water, and beat again. Add the prunes to the batter, and mix well.

Spoon the batter into a frying pan with heated fat. Fry on both sides until golden brown.

Serve them hot, sprinkled with powdered sugar, along with sweet milk, coffee, or tea.

Barley Porridge

Miežienė

*2 cups barley groats,
1 cup water, 1 cup milk,
100 g butter, salt.*

Soak the groats in water for a few hours. After soaking, put the groats into boiling water, and cook until tender. Then add the milk, salt, and butter, stirring to prevent burning.

Barley Porridge with Cottage Cheese

Miežienė su varške

*3 cups barley groats,
400 g cottage cheese, 3 eggs,
300 g butter, 100 g sour cream,
1 tsp marjoram, salt,
3 cups water.*

Soak the groats in water for 2 hrs. After soaking, pour the groats into boiling water, and cook until tender.

Add 3 tablespoons of the butter and the eggs to the cottage cheese, and mix well. Then add the porridge, chopped marjoram, and salt, mixing thoroughly.

Pour this mixture into a greased baking pan sprinkled with flour. Put several pats of butter on top, and bake in a moderate oven (180 °C) for 20–25 min.

Serve hot with melted butter and sour cream, along with milk.

Barley Porridge with Grated Potatoes

Miežienė su bulvių tarkiais

*3 cups fine barley groats,
3 cups water, 3 cups finely
grated potatoes, 200 g butter,
2 onions, dill sprigs, salt.*

Pour hot water over the groat, and soak for 2 hrs. After soaking, cook the groats over a low flame in the same water which they were soaked in until tender. Then while constantly stirring, add the grated potatoes and salt. Continue cooking for 10–15 min. while constantly stirring to prevent burning.

After cooking, pour the porridge into an earthenware bowl, and add finely chopped onions sautéed in butter. Sprinkle with chopped dill.

Serve with sweet or sour milk or with poppy seed milk.

Crushed Barley
Porridge with Potatoes

Grucė su bulvėmis

2 cups crushed pearl barley,
1 l water, 1 l milk, ½ kg potatoes,
100 g butter, ½ tsp tarragon, salt.
FOR THE SAUCE:
150 g butter, 2 onions,
3 tbsps sour cream.

Pour hot water over the barley, and soak for 2–3 hrs. After soaking, cook the barley over a low flame in the same water in which it was soaked, until it begins to thicken. Then add warmed milk, peeled and thinly sliced potatoes, butter, salt, and chopped tarragon, and while constantly stirring, cook until the potatoes are completely tender.

After cooking, spoon the porridge into a bowl, pour over with finely chopped onions sautéed in butter, and add sour cream.

Crushed Barley
Porridge with Herring

Grucė su silkėmis

3 cups pearl barley,
3 cups water, 2 herring,
2 onions, 3 tbsps cooking oil.

Pour hot water over the barley, and soak very well.

Peel the herring, remove the bones, cut into small pieces, and put into a pot. To the same pot also add finely chopped onions, cooking oil, the soaked barley, and water, mixing well. Cover and bake in an oven until the barley is tender.

Serve hot with bread or potatoes.

Serve at the table from the same pot in which it was baked.

Half-and-Half Porridge

Pusinė košė

3 cups barley or rye flour,
½ kg potatoes, ½ l milk,
1 tsp tarragon, salt, water.

Peel the potatoes, cover with water, and boil until they begin to crack. Then pour the liquid from the potatoes into a bowl, and mash the potatoes in the same pot until they form a pliable mass.

Into this mass pour the liquid from the potatoes and milk, the tarragon, and mix thoroughly, and cook again while constantly stirring to prevent burning. When the porridge begins to boil, add the flour in a thin stream while straining it with your fingers to keep out lumps. Stir vigorously continuously. Add just enough flour so that when the porridge comes to a boil (and that takes 10–15 min.), a normal thickness remains.

After cooking, spoon the porridge into a bowl, and in the middle make a small indentation into which melted butter and sour cream sauce may be poured.

Serve hot with sweet or sour milk. Poppy seed milk also goes very well with this porridge.

Buckwheat Porridge

Grikių košė

2 cups buckwheat groats,
2 cups milk, 1 cup water,
200 g butter, 1 onion.

Soak the buckwheat in water for a few hours. After soaking, pour into boiling water, and cook until it begins to thicken. Then add the milk, and continue cooking until the buckwheat absorbs all of the liquid. Then add a finely chopped onion sautéed in butter, the remaining butter, salt, and mix well. Cover and put into a warm oven to bake for a while.

Serve with warm milk.

Buckwheat Pasties with Mushrooms

Grikių pyragėliai su grybais

2 cups fine buckwheat groats,
2 cups milk, 2 cups water,
2 eggs, 4 tbsps wheat flour,
20 g butter, cooking fat, salt.
FOR THE FILLING:
30 g dried mushrooms,
30 g butter, 1 onion, 2 tbsps sour
cream, 1 tbsp dried bread crumbs,
1 tbsp lemon-balm leaves, salt.
FOR THE SAUCE:
3 onions, 30 g butter, 2 tbsps flour,
½ cup sour cream, mushroom broth,
parsley sprigs, dill sprigs, salt.

Pour the buckwheat groats into boiling water, and cook over a low flame until they begin to thicken (for 15–20 min.). Then add the milk, butter, and salt, and cook until the buckwheat absorbs the liquid. Add the flour and eggs to the buckwheat after it has cooled off, and knead into a dough of medium stiffness.

To make the filling, cook the mushrooms after soaking, slice thinly, sauté in butter with finely chopped onions. Add the sour cream, chopped lemon balm, dried bread crumbs, and salt, mixing well.

Tear off a walnut-sized piece of dough, flatten thinly on the palm of your hand, put a tablespoon of mushroom filling in the middle, fold the edges, and make a small pasty. Fry the pasties in a frying pan in a large amount of heated fat. Serve with onion sauce.

To make the sauce, cut the onions into thin slices, sauté in butter, add the flour, cook for 2–3 min., add some mushroom broth, cook for 1–2 min., add chopped dill and parsley leaves, add the sour cream, and heat again, but do not bring to a boil.

Buckwheat pasties are a holiday food in the Dzūkija region.

Buckwheat Squares

Grikių apkepas

3 cups buckwheat flour, 2 eggs,
2 cups sour milk, 100 g butter,
1 onion, ½ tsp baking soda, salt.

Mix the flour with the baking soda. Sauté a finely chopped onion in butter, and add to the flour. Then add the milk, eggs, salt, and mix well into a somewhat thick dough.

Spoon this dough into a greased baking pan sprinkled with flour, and bake in a moderate oven (180 °C) until the top turns golden brown (for 30–45 min.).

After baking, slice the buckwheat into squares, place into a deep dish, add melted butter and sour cream.

Serve with sour milk or with sweetened water.

Grikainiai

Buckwheat Pancakes

3 cups buckwheat flour,
2 cups sour milk or buttermilk,
1 egg, 2 tbsps sour cream,
1 tsp crushed mint, salt,
cooking fat.

Mix the flour with the sour milk, add the egg, sour cream, chopped mint, and salt. Combine the ingredients, and beat very well into a batter with the consistency of sour cream.

In heated fat, fry small pancakes (each from 1 tbsp of batter).

Serve buckwheat pancakes hot with sugar, sour cream, or berry preserves.

Avižinė košė

Oat Porridge

1 cup oat groats, 2 cups milk,
2 tbsps butter, 1 tsp sugar, salt.

Add the oat groats to boiling milk. Cook over a low flame, while constantly stirring. After cooking for 10 min., add the butter, sugar, and salt. Mix well, cover the pot, and remove from the heat. Let stand for several minutes for the porridge to absorb the liquid.

Serve with sweet milk.

Avižinis kisielius

Oat Kisiel

½ kg coarsely ground or rolled oats,
2–3 crusts black rye bread,
3 pieces charred wood or 3 carbon
tablets, 1½ l water, salt.

Pour the oatmeal into 1 l warm water (35–40 °C) and mix well. Add several crusts of black rye bread to improve fermentation. Also add some pieces of charred birch to draw the bitterness out of the oats. Put in a warm place, and keep for 12–14 hrs. to ferment. Pour off the liquid after the mixture has settled, pour ½ l water over the fermented oatmeal, strain through a sieve. Pour this liquid into a pot, add salt, and while constantly stirring, cook until it thickens (for 5–8 min.). After cooking, pour the liquid into a bowl, and put in a cold place for several hours to set.

Serve kisiel with potatoes and sweetened water or sugar, or with poppy seed or hemp seed milk and honey.

When making oat kisiel, birch or maple sap may be used instead of water. Then it has a sweet and sour flavor and is much tastier.

Čiulkis

Mashed Hemp Seed

1 cup hemp seed, 1 apple,
1 slice bread without the crust, salt.

Mash the hemp seed well, add slices of a well-ripened peeled apple and the bread without the crust, and mash well once more.

Make little balls from this dough. When eating, serve with herbal tea, poppy seed or hemp seed milk, or acorn or grain coffee.

Mashed hemp seed was usually enjoyed by children.

Another name for čiulkis is grūstinis (which also refers to a mashed food).

Hemp Seed Porridge

Kanapienė

*1 cup hemp seed, 1 onion,
3 tbsps flour, 1½ cups water,
pepper, salt.*

Fry the hemp seed in a frying pan, and while still hot, grind into flour.

Pour 3 tablespoons of flour into boiling water, stirring to prevent burning, add a finely chopped onion, ground pepper, and salt, and while stirring, cook over a low flame for 5–8 min. Remove from the fire, add the hemp seed flour, mix well.

Serve hot as a side dish with boiled or baked potatoes in their skins.

This food is popular in the Žemaitija region.

Hemp Seed Soup

Kanapių putra

*1 cup hemp seed, 1 onion,
1 cup water, 25 g butter or
cooking oil, pepper, salt.*

Fry the hemp seed in a frying pan, and grind into flour. Finely chop the onion, and sauté in butter or cooking oil.

While stirring to prevent burning, pour the hemp seed flour into boiling water, add the sautéed onion, ground pepper, and salt. While stirring, heat to boiling.

Hemp seed soup should be much thinner than hemp seed porridge (which contains flour).

Serve with bread.

Hemp Seed Spread

Kanapių tyrė

*2 cups hemp seed,
2 onions, salt.*

Mash the hemp seed together with finely chopped onions and salt.

Spread the hemp seed mixture on slices of bread, and bake in an oven (for 5–10 min.). Serve hot in the afternoon with kvass or tea.

Use hemp seed spread as a filling for grated or boiled potatoes and for pasties. It can also be used to flavor other dishes.

Hemp Seed Tobacco

Kanapių tabokas

*1 cup hemp seed,
1 onion, salt.*

Fry the hemp seed in a frying pan together with a chopped onion, and add salt. Fry until it begins to brown. Then pour into a mortar and mash.

Hemp seed tobacco is also called kanapių druska (hemp seed salt), spirgynė (sizzled hemp seed), spirgiukai (sizzled hemp seed), kanapiai (hemp seed), and grūdinys (mash).

Serve potatoes with hemp seed tobacco. You can also use it to add flavor to potato, herring, vegetable, egg, and other dishes.

Hemp Seed Milk

Kanapių pienas

*½ l hemp seed,
1 l boiled water.*

Wash the hemp seed, drain, and toast for 3–5 min. in a frying pan. While the hemp seed is still hot, pour into a mortar and grind into flour. Pour the ground hemp seed into a bowl, add hot boiled water, mix well, pour into a cloth bag, and squeeze out. Pour water over the hemp seed, and squeeze out a few more times.

Use hemp seed milk to flavor cabbage, groats, beet soup, and other soups. Hemp seed milk goes well with potatoes and oat kisiel (after it has been seasoned with onions, pepper, and salt) or instead of a sauce with dumplings, boiled dough squares, and pasties.

Hemp Seed Curd

Kanapių varškė

1 l hemp seed milk

Pour the hemp seed milk into a pot, and heat very slowly until it curdles. When curds form, pour off the liquid.

Add hemp seed curd as a filling to potato or flour dumplings.

From this curd, hemp seed cheese can be made: knead the curd with bread (after removing the crust), and make little dumplings. Serve with poppy seed or hemp seed milk or with sweet milk.

Hemp Seed Brine

Kanapių rasalas

1 herring, ½ l hemp seed milk, 1 onion.

Peel the herring, remove the bones, fry, and cut into small pieces. Put the pieces of herring into a bowl, add a finely chopped onion, and mash with a wooden spoon. Add the hemp seed milk, and mix well.

Serve with hot boiled or baked potatoes in their skins.

Poppy Seed Milk

Aguonų pienas

*1 cup poppy seeds,
1 l water, ½ cup sugar.*

Pour boiling water over the poppy seeds, and let stand for 2–3 hrs. so that they swell up. Then pour off the water, mash the poppy seeds well, or grind with a meat grinder 2–3 times, add 1 liter of boiled cold water, mix well. Strain through a cloth. Sweeten the liquid.

Serve poppy seed milk with various pastries. It can be used to make soups, various beverages and sauces.

Baked Peas or Broad Beans

Kepti žirniai ar pupos

*1 l peas or broad beans,
3–4 juniper berries, 1 sprig
oregano, 1 tsp sage, salt.*

Soak the broad beans or peas in water for 10-12 hrs. After soaking, pour into an earthenware pot, add the seasonings and salt. Stuff the pot with pea stalks so that nothing falls out. Turn the pot upside down, put into a hot oven, and bake for 45–60 min. Carefully remove the pot from the oven, remove the pea stalks, pour the baked broad beans or peas into a bowl, and put in a windy place so that they split.

Boiled Peas or Broad Beans

Virti žirniai ar pupos

*1 l peas or broad beans,
½ cup caraway seeds, salt.*

Soak the broad beans or peas (for 10–12 hrs.), and boil in well-salted water over a low flame (use enough water to cover the peas or beans).

After boiling, pour off the remaining water, sprinkle caraway seeds over the beans or peas, and shake well so that they gain a floury texture.

Pour into an earthenware bowl, and serve with beer. A mixture of peas and beans may also be served with beer. Boiled peas or beans can also be served with sauerkraut, or serve with other dishes instead of bread. Serve poured over with hemp seed milk.

Broad Beans with Horseradish

Pupos su krienais

*1 l boiled broad beans, 1 cup sour cream,
3 tbsps finely grated horseradish,
100 g green onions or chives, salt.*

Cut the boiled broad beans into halves, pour into a bowl, add the horseradish, sour cream, and salt. Mix well. Sprinkle with chopped green onions or chives.

Garlic Broad Beans

Pupų česnakynė

*10-12 cloves garlic, 1 cup boiled
broad beans, 2 carrots, 200 g sour
cream, dill sprigs, salt.*

Peel the garlic cloves, and chop finely, peel the boiled broad beans, and cut into halves. Peel and finely grate the carrots. Put everything into a bowl, add sour cream and salt, mix well, sprinkle with chopped dill.

Pea Balls

Čiulkinys

*1 l peas, 2 onions,
1 tsp tarragon,
2 tbsps butter, salt.*

Soak the peas well, and boil with the tarragon, pour off the water, mash. Add onions sautéed in butter, add salt, knead well, and afterwards make little balls. Serve hot or cold with sour or sweet milk, buttermilk, or poppy seed milk.

Pea Porridge

Žirnių košė

½ l peas, 1 tbsp flour,
100 g butter, 2 onions, salt.

Soak the peas well, pour into a pot, and add cold water (enough to cover the peas). Cook over a low flame until tender. Then, while stirring, add the flour and salt, continue cooking for 3–5 min.

After cooking, spoon the porridge into a bowl, add finely chopped onions sautéed in butter.

Serve with sour or sweet milk.

Broad Bean Porridge

Pupų košė

½ l broad beans,
3 medium-sized potatoes,
1 cup milk, 100 g butter,
2 onions, 1 tsp tarragon,
2 tbsps caraway seeds, salt.

Soak the broad beans well, pour into a pot, add cold water to cover them completely, and cook over a low flame until tender.

Mash the tender beans, add the milk, finely grated potatoes, add the spices and salt. While stirring with a wooden spatula or wooden spoon, cook until the grated potatoes no longer crunch between your teeth when tasting them.

After cooking, spoon the porridge into a bowl, and add finely chopped onions sautéed in butter.

Serve hot with sour milk, buttermilk, or kvass.

Stewed Broad Beans

Troškintos pupos

2 cups broad beans,
1 tbsp caraway seeds,
1 cup sour cream, 1 carrot,
100 g butter, 1 tsp oregano,
parsley leaves, salt.

Soak the broad beans well (for 10–12 hrs.), add water, and cook. Pour off the water, peel, and put into a pot. Add butter, a coarsely grated carrot, sour cream, caraway seeds, oregano, and salt, stew over a low flame until the grated carrot is tender.

Spoon the porridge into a bowl, and sprinkle with parsley leaves.

Serve with sweet milk.

Broad Bean Balls

Pupinukai

2 cups broad beans,
1 cup flour, 1 egg,
1 onion, 100 g butter,
100 g sour cream,
1 tsp sage, salt.

Soak the broad beans well, cook, mash, add the flour, chopped sage, and egg, and knead into a dough. From this dough make little round balls, put into boiling salted water, and cook for 5–7 min. Remove the broad bean balls from the pot, put into an earthenware bowl.

Sauté a finely chopped onion in butter, add the sour cream, and pour this sauce over the broad bean balls.

Pea Fingers

Gurguzai

1 l peas, 2 onions,
3 tbsps butter, 1 tsp sage
or oregano, salt.
FOR THE SAUCE:
100 g butter,
100 g sour cream.

Soak the peas well, and cook in salted water over a low flame (use enough water to cover the peas).

When the peas are tender, pour off the water, mash the peas in the same pot, sprinkle with sage or oregano, add finely chopped onions sautéed in butter. Add salt. Knead well. Take a heaping tablespoon of the mixture, put on the palm of your hand, and make oblong fingers. Put the fingers into a pot, pour melted butter and sour cream over them. Cover the pot, and put in a hot oven (220 °C) to bake lightly.

Serve hot.

Boiled Broad Bean Pods

Virtos pupų ankštys

1 l broad bean pods,
1 l water, dill, salt.

Boil the raw broad bean pods in salted water with dill until tender. After boiling, drain.

After peeling off the pods, eat the beans as an afternoon snack or serve with beer.

Garden Beans with Onions

Pupelės su svogūnais

1 cup cooked garden beans,
50 g fat (butter or cooking oil),
1 onion, 2 tbsps sour
cream, 1 tbsp flour.

Sauté a finely chopped onion in fat, add sour cream beaten with flour, mix well, and cook for 3–5 min.

Pour this sauce over the garden beans, and mix well.

Serve with hot potatoes.

Pea Cakes

Žirnių raguoliai

3 cups coarsely ground
pea flour, water, salt.
FOR THE SAUCE:
2 boiled potatoes,
100 g butter, 1 egg,
½ cup milk, 1 onion,
dill sprigs, salt.

Pour the flour into a large earthenware bowl, add water and salt, and mix into a batter thicker than what is made for pancakes. Beat until it becomes white and porous, filling up with bubbles. Batter beaten this way in a bowl rises a great deal. Then spoon the batter into a greased baking pan, and bake in a hot oven until it turns golden brown (for 15–20 min.).

Serve hot with sour milk and sauce.

To make the sauce, mash the boiled potatoes, add the egg, and mix well. Sauté a finely chopped onion in butter, add the potato mixture and chopped dill, mix well, add warmed milk, and while constantly stirring, heat for 3–5 min.

Pea cakes are a breakfast food in the Aukštaitija region.

Šilkinė košė | Silk Porridge

1 cup peas, 3 medium-sized potatoes, 1½ l water, 1 tsp sage, salt.
FOR THE SAUCE:
100 g butter.

Soak the peas well, add water, and cook over a low flame until tender. To the tender peas add finely grated potatoes, salt, and chopped sage, continue cooking while stirring until the porridge thickens and the grated potato does not crunch between your teeth when tasted.

Serve with melted butter and sweet or sour milk, kvass, or beer.

Žirninis paplotis | Pea Cake

3 cups pea flour, water, salt.
FOR THE SAUCE:
200 g cottage cheese, 200 g butter, mint leaves, salt.

Mix the flour and salted water into a somewhat thick batter (thicker than that made for pancakes). Beat until it becomes white and porous, filling up with bubbles.

Spoon the batter into a greased baking pan sprinkled with flour, and bake in an oven for 45–50 min.

To make the sauce, mash the cottage cheese with chopped mint, add hot melted butter and salt, mix well, and heat in an oven for 5–10 min.

Serve pea cake as soon as it is removed from the oven. After cooling, it becomes hard and is no longer tasty.

This is a breakfast food in the Aukštaitija region.

Žirniniai blynai | Pea Pancakes

3 cups pea flour, 4 cups whey, salt, cooking fat.
FOR THE SAUCE:
200 g cottage cheese, 100 g butter, 50 g sour cream, salt.

Mix a batter from the flour and whey, and beat very well, adding salt. Put this batter into a frying pan with heated fat, and fry until a crust forms on both sides.

To make the sauce, mash the cottage cheese with sour cream, add salt and melted butter, heat in an oven.

Serve hot with hot cottage cheese.

vegetables
and fruits

Pickled Red Beets

For pickling, select small beets of a uniform size. Peel, wash, and put into a wooden, earthenware, enamel, or glass crock, along with cold salted water (1 tsp salt per 1 l water), and adding several crusts of black bread. Spread cheesecloth over the crock, cover with a board, press down with weights, and let pickle. At first, keep at room temperature until the pickling process begins. Later, put into a cool room, but do not freeze.

Use after 1–2 weeks. While pickling, do not let the edges of the crock get over-grown with mould. If mould appears, clean off the edges of the crock, wash off the board and the cheesecloth, and again use weights to press down the board.

If you want pickled beets in 4–5 days, then cut into thin slices or strips – they will pickle faster.

Pickle these beets in a cool place. They can be kept for a whole year.

From pickled beets, one can make soups, salads, and other dishes.

Use beet brine (rasalas) as a natural acid when making soups as well as fish, vegetable, and other dishes and beverages. After straining and salting, beet brine can be used to make a beverage with a distinctive taste and beautiful colour. The curative properties of beet brine are well known and valued: people drink it to recover from illnesses and inflammations, and to strengthen their immune systems and blood.

Pickled Boiled Beets

Boil and peel the beets, cover with cold water (1 tsp salt per 1 l water), add several crusts of black rye bread, press down with weights, and set the crock in a warm place. After 3–4 days the beets are sweet and sour and ready to be eaten.

They are not suitable for keeping a long time and so are pickled in small quantities.

Beets with Broad Beans

2 medium-sized boiled pickled beets, ½ l boiled broad beans, 3 onions, 3–4 crushed juniper berries, ½ tsp chopped calendula, 5 tbsps cooking oil, 1 tbsp caraway seeds, salt.

Finely dice the beets. Peel the broad beans, and cut into halves. Slice the onions, sauté in oil, and add the seasonings while sautéing.

Add the sliced beans, sautéed onions, and salt to the diced beets. Mix everything thoroughly, and sprinkle with caraway seeds washed in boiling water and with crushed calendula.

Beet Salad

Burokėlių salotos

2 boiled pickled beets, 4 tbsps cooking oil, 3 onions, ¼ tsp ground pepper, chopped garlic, chives, salt.

Finely dice the beets. Slice the onions, sauté in oil. Put everything into a bowl, sprinkle with pepper, and add chopped chives, salt, and mix thoroughly.

Serve this salad with potatoes, or serve with other dishes.

Beets with Horseradish

Burokėliai su krienais

4 boiled pickled beets, 1 cup grated horseradish, 5 tbsps cooking oil or 200 g sour cream, salt.

Finely grate the beets, adding the finely grated horseradish, oil or sour cream, and salt. Mix everything thoroughly.

Serve this beet salad with other dishes, or eat with hot potatoes or bread.

Beets with Caraway Seeds

Burokėliai su kmynais

3 boiled pickled beets, 3 tbsps caraway seeds, 1 tsp sugar, 100 g sour cream, salt.

Finely dice the beets. Pour a cup of water over the caraway seeds, boil for 5 min. Let cool, strain, and pour the caraway seeds over the diced beets. Add sugar and salt, and let stand for 3 hrs. Before eating, pour off the liquid from the beets, add sour cream, and mix thoroughly.

Serve with potatoes, or with other dishes.

Beets with Herring

Burokėliai su silke

2 boiled beets, 2 onions, 1 cup sauerkraut juice, 2 smoked herrings, ½ tsp sugar.

Peel the boiled beets, and grate coarsely, adding strained sauerkraut juice, sugar, and finely sliced onions.

Peel the herring, remove the bones, and slice finely, adding to the beets. Mix thoroughly.

Serve this salad with black bread fried in oil.

Nobleman's Bacon

Bajoro lašiniai

3 boiled pickled beets, 2 herrings, 1 cup beet brine, 1 onion, 1 tbsp caraway seeds, 1 tsp oregano.

Dice the beets. Peel the herring, remove the bones, and cut up. Put the diced beets and herring into a pan, sprinkle with caraway seeds, sliced onions, and chopped oregano, and pour over with beet brine. Stew in an oven for 10–15 min.

Serve with potatoes or bread.

Beets with Poppy Seed Milk

Burokėliai su aguonų pienu

2 boiled pickled beets,
1 cup poppy seeds,
1 l water, salt.

Pour boiling water over the poppy seeds, and let stand for 2–3 hrs. so that they swell up. Then pour off the water, mash the poppy seeds well, or grind with a meat grinder 2–3 times, add 1 l of boiled water, and strain through a cloth.

Finely dice the beets, adding the poppy seed milk and salt.

Serve with baked potatoes.

Coleslaw

Šviežių kopūstų salotos

400 g cabbage, 1 carrot,
50 g green onions,
borage leaves, dill sprigs,
200 g sour cream, salt.

Shred the cabbage and put into a bowl. Sprinkle with salt, and rub with a wooden spoon. Add a coarsely grated carrot to the cabbage, and add finely chopped green onions, dill sprigs, borage leaves, and sour cream. Mix thoroughly.

Serve this salad as soon as it is prepared.

Serve with hot potatoes (it is especially delicious when they are fresh), or serve with other dishes.

Stuffed Cabbage Head

Įdaryta kopūsto gūžė

1 kg head of cabbage (fresh or pickled),
1 l fresh or salted mushrooms,
3 onions, 100 g butter,
½ cup milk, 4 slices bread,
3 eggs, 3 cloves garlic,
¼ tsp ground pepper,
1 cup sour cream,
parsley sprigs, salt.

Put the head of cabbage into boiling salted water, and boil for 10–15 min. After removing, pour cold water over it, drain, and let cool. Carefully spread out the cabbage leaves, and spread a thin layer of the filling over them.

To make the filling, partially cook the fresh mushrooms. If salted are being used, soak and wash very well. Finely chop the mushrooms. To the mushrooms, add the slices of bread after soaking them in milk. Add the finely chopped onions sautéed in butter, pepper, finely chopped garlic, eggs, and salt, mixing well.

Firmly squeeze together the stuffed head of cabbage (to restore the form of the head), put into a greased baking pan, add 1 cup of water, and bake in a hot oven for about 30 min. until the head of cabbage turns golden brown. Then pour sour cream over the top, cover, and stew for 10–15 more min.

Put the baked head of cabbage into a small bowl carefully cut up (so that it does not fall apart), pour the sauce in which it was stewed over it. Sprinkle with chopped parsley sprigs.

Serve hot with hot baked potatoes.

Stuffed Cabbage with Mushrooms

Balandėliai su grybais

1 kg head of cabbage (fresh or pickled), 1 cup salted or 100 g dried mushrooms, 1 onion, 1 egg, 2 tbsps bread crumbs, 50 g butter, 1 tsp oregano, pepper, dill sprigs, salt, 200 g sour cream.

Cut out the stem from the cabbage head and put into boiling salted water, cooking for 10–15 min. Individually separate the leaves from the partially cooked head, cutting out the thicker parts.

If salted mushrooms are being used, soak well, and wash. If dried mushrooms are used, soak for 2–3 hrs., and boil in the same water in which they were soaked.

Finely chop the onion, and sauté in butter. When the onion is almost done, add finely sliced mushrooms, and sauté for 2–3 min. more. Add the bread crumbs, a beaten egg, ground pepper, chopped oregano, and salt, mixing well.

Put some of the mushroom filling on each cabbage leaf, and roll into the shape of an envelope, folding over the ends.

Put the stuffed cabbages into a pan, pouring water over the cabbages, and stew for 30–35 min. When they are almost done, add the sour cream.

After removing the stuffed cabbages from the flame, carefully put into a bowl, pour the liquid in which they were stewed over them. Sprinkle with chopped dill.

Sauerkraut

Rauginti kopūstai

10 kg cabbage, ½ kg carrots, 1 cup caraway seeds, 200 g salt, 100 g sugar, ½ l cranberries, 15 juniper berries.

Wash out a wooden, enamel, or earthenware crock, and line the clean bottom with cabbage leaves. Cut the cabbage, and mix thoroughly with coarsely grated carrots and the other ingredients, pouring them into the crock and filling it to a depth of 20–25 cm, and then mashing everything. Keep adding in this way until the crock is almost full (leaving 10 cm to the top). Spread the cheesecloth over the top, cover with a lid, and press down with weights. Above the lid there should be a layer of juice 2–3 cm deep. At first, ferment at a temperature of 16–20 °C. After 3 days take the cover off the cabbage, and stick a wooden rod all the way to the bottom in order to release the gas formed during fermentation. After a further 5 to 6 days and after cleaning off the surface and compressing well, press the sauerkraut down again with weights, and place in a cold room (the temperature can be as low as -5 °C). Check the sauerkraut often for mould. Wash the lid and cheesecloth, cleaning off the edges of the crock.

When making sauerkraut, homemakers often put small whole heads of cabbage into the bottom of the barrel. After fermentation, they are used to make salads and other dishes.

It is said that each cook has his or her own pickling recipe. What must be included are salt and carrots. If the cabbages are being fermented earlier or there is no cold place to keep them, it is not advisable to add sugar, as the sauerkraut will have a mushy texture. Cranberries with apples or with caraway seeds may be added as well as juniper berries or nigella seeds.

Cabbage with Beet Brine

Kopūstai rasale

1 small head of cabbage,
1 tbsp caraway seeds,
1 cup beet brine,
green onions, salt.

Boil the head of cabbage in salted water for 15–20 min. Remove and drain. Put the cooked head into a bowl, carefully cut into four parts, and pour beet brine over it. Sprinkle with sliced green onions and caraway seeds.

Serve with hot potatoes.

Sauerkraut Salad with Horseradish

Kopūstų
salotos su krienais

½ l sauerkraut, 1 cup sour cream,
2 tbsps grated horseradish,
1 onion, 1 tsp sugar, salt.

Add the finely grated horseradish to the sauerkraut, sprinkling with sugar. Add a finely chopped onion, sour cream, and salt. Mix everything thoroughly.

Serve with hot potatoes, or serve with other dishes.

Sauerkraut Salad with Onions

Kopūstų salotos su svogūnais

½ l sauerkraut,
4 onions, ½ tsp sage,
100 g cooking oil.

Put the sauerkraut into a bowl.

Finely chop the onions, sauté in oil with chopped sage leaves, and pour over the sauerkraut. Let stand for 2–3 hrs. so that the sauerkraut absorbs the oil.

Serve this sauerkraut salad with potatoes boiled in their skins, or serve with other dishes.

Sauerkraut and Broad Bean Salad

Kopūstų ir pupų salotos

½ l sauerkraut,
½ l boiled broad beans,
1 cup cooking oil, 1 herring,
2 onions, 1 tsp caraway seeds,
1 tsp sugar, juniper berries, salt.

If the sauerkraut is very sour, wash first, then sprinkle with sugar, adding the beans and mixing thoroughly. Slice the onions and sauté in oil. Then, while they are still hot, pour in the sauerkraut and bean mixture, adding the caraway seeds and ground juniper berries. Peel the herring, remove the bones, and cut into slices, and add to the sauerkraut. Mix everything thoroughly.

Serve with hot boiled or baked potatoes.

Stewed Sauerkraut

Troškinti rauginti kopūstai

½ l sauerkraut, 150 g cooking oil
or butter, 2 onions.

Wash the sauerkraut if it is sour, and put into a pot, adding sliced onions sautéed in fat, and the remaining fat. If caraway seeds were not added to the sauerkraut during fermentation, now add 1 tbsp. Cover the pot, and stew over a low flame or in an oven until tender (for 25–30 min.).

Serve stewed sauerkraut with hot potatoes, or with other dishes.

Sauerkraut Stewed with Mushrooms

Kopūstai,
troškinti su grybais

*½ l sauerkraut, 1 cup fresh, pickled,
salted, or dried mushrooms,
2 onions, 200 g butter or
cooking oil, salt.*

If the mushrooms are salted, soak well and wash. If dried mushrooms are being used, soak for 2–3 hrs., and boil in the same water in which they were soaked.

Wash the sauerkraut if it is sour, put into a pot, adding finely chopped onions sautéed in fat, sliced mushrooms, and the remaining fat. If boiled dried mushrooms are being used, also add the liquid in which they were boiled. Add salt. Cover the pot, and stew over a low flame or in an oven for 30–35 min.

Serve stewed sauerkraut with hot potatoes or bread.

Pickles

Rauginti agurkai

*10 kg small autumn cucumbers,
5 cloves garlic, 100 g horseradish
leaves, 300 g ripe dill with all the
seeds, 100 g black currant
leaves, 50 g oak leaves,
10–12 juniper berries, salt.*

Line the bottom of a clean wooden, earthenware, or enamel crock with spices, arranging a layer of cucumbers and then one of spices until the crock is almost full. The top layer must be of spices. It is not necessary to use all the spices in the quantities shown. It is up to the preparer to decide which ones should be used.

Pour a salt solution over the cucumbers. For immediate use (after 2–3 days), add 300 g of salt to 10 l of water. If pickling for the winter, add 700 g of salt to 10 l of cold water. After pouring over with the salt solution, press the cucumbers down with a lid, and immediately place in a cool room. But even after the cucumbers are completely pickled, do not freeze.

Horseradish Sauce

Krienų padažas

*½ cup grated horseradish,
200 g sour cream,
1 tbsp sugar, salt.*

Mix the sour cream with the fresh, finely grated horseradish, adding the sugar and salt, and mixing thoroughly.

If a weaker and thinner sauce is desired, add more sour cream.

Hot Horseradish Sauce

Karštas krienų padažas

*3 tbsps grated horseradish,
20 g butter, 1 tbsp flour,
1 cup pickled beet brine,
½ cup sour cream,
1 tsp sugar, salt.*

In melted butter briefly fry the flour for 3 min., add the finely grated horseradish, beet brine, sugar, and salt, mixing thoroughly, bringing it to a boil over a low flame.

At the end add the sour cream and mix thoroughly. Heat, but do not bring to a boil.

Black Radish Salad

Juodųjų ridikų salotos

2 medium-sized black radishes, 200 g sour cream, 8–10 dill sprigs, salt.

Peel the radishes, wash, cut into very thin slices, sprinkle with salt, and after covering with another bowl, shake to soften. Add the sour cream and salt, mixing thoroughly. Sprinkle with chopped dill.

Serve with hot boiled or baked potatoes, or with other dishes.

Turnip Salad

Ropių salotos

1 medium-sized turnip, 100 g green onions, 8–10 dill sprigs, 200 g sour cream, salt.

Peel the turnip, wash, and coarsely grate. Cover with another bowl, and shake well. Add the sour cream, sliced green onions, chopped dill, and salt. Mix thoroughly.

Serve with potatoes in the afternoon, or with other dishes.

Rutabaga Salad

Griežčių salotos

1 rutabaga, 200 g sour cream, 100 g green onions, dill sprigs, salt.

Peel the rutabaga, wash, and coarsely grate. Cover with another bowl, and shake. Add finely sliced green onions, dill, salt, and sour cream. Mix thoroughly.

Serve with bread, or with other dishes.

Rutabagas with Carrots

Griežčiai su morkomis

2 cups coarsely grated rutabaga, 1 cup coarsely grated carrots, 1 clove garlic, dill sprigs, leeks, salt.

Grate the rutabagas and carrots, and put into a bowl, adding salt. Cover with a bowl, and shake well. Then add finely chopped garlic and leeks, adding sour cream and mixing everything thoroughly. Put into a bowl, and sprinkle with chopped dill.

Serve this salad with other dishes, or serve in the afternoon with baked potatoes.

Tomatoes Stuffed with Rutabagas

Griežčiais įdaryti pomidorai

5 tomatoes, ½ l coarsely grated rutabagas, ½ cup sour cream, dill sprigs, green onions, salt.

Cut each tomato in half, scooping out the insides. Add salt to the rutabagas, cover with another bowl, and shake vigorously to soften. Add finely sliced green onions and sour cream, mixing thoroughly. Put the tomatoes on a plate, filling each with the rutabaga mixture. Sprinkle with chopped dill.

Serve with fried garlic bread.

Carrots with Garlic

Morkos su česnaku

2–3 carrots, 2 tsps crushed garlic, ½ cup sour cream, salt.

Grate the carrots into long thin shreds, adding the garlic and salt, and mixing thoroughly. Leave in a cool place for a few hours. Before eating, add the sour cream. Mix thoroughly.

Serve with fried bread, or with other dishes.

Radish Salad

Ridikėlių salotos

400 g radishes, 2 hard-boiled eggs, 200 g sour cream, 100 g green onions, dill sprigs, salt.

Wash the radishes, cutting into thin slices. Add finely sliced green onions, sour cream, and salt, mixing well.

Put the radish mixture into a salad bowl, top with wedges of hard-boiled egg, and sprinkle with chopped dill.

Can be served as a snack, or with other dishes.

Black Salsify Salad

Gelteklių salotos

3 black salsify roots, 1 cup cubes of dried black bread, 1 cup sour cream, chopped dill, salt.

Thoroughly clean the black salsify roots, wash, and cut into thin slices.

Put the bread cubes, slices of black salsify, and salt into a bowl, pouring sour cream over the mixture. Sprinkle with chopped dill.

Fresh Vegetable Salad

Šviežių daržovių salotos

200 g leaf lettuce, 8-10 radishes, 2 cucumbers, 100 g green onions, dill sprigs, 200 g sour cream, salt.

Thinly slice the radishes, dice the cucumbers, and chop the lettuce leaves, dill, and slice the green onions. Put everything into a bowl, adding the sour cream and salt, and mixing thoroughly.

Serve with hot boiled or baked potatoes, or with other dishes.

Onion Salad

Svogūnų salotos

3 onions, 1 carrot, 3 tbsps cooking oil or butter, a bit of ground pepper, lovage leaves, salt.

Slice the onions. Heat the oil or butter in a frying pan, add the pepper, lovage leaves, coarsely grated carrot, and salt, and sauté briefly for 5 min. Pour the hot grated carrot over the sliced onions.

After the salad has cooled, eat with fried bread, or serve with herring or other fish dishes.

Onion Salad with Beets

Svogūnų salotos su burokėliais

4 onions, 2 small boiled pickled beets, 1 cup beet brine, a bit of ground pepper, 2-3 juniper berries, ½ tsp sugar, salt.

Slice the onions, and put into a bowl. Thinly slice the beets, and arrange over the onions. Pour strained beet brine over everything, and sprinkle with sugar, pepper, crushed juniper berries, and salt. Let stand for 2-3 hrs.

Serve onion salad prepared in this way with hot baked or boiled potatoes, or with other dishes.

Onions Stuffed with Mushrooms

Grybais įdaryti svogūnai

2 large onions, 2 cups boiled or salted mushrooms, 1 egg, 1 cup sour cream, 2 tbsps butter, 3 peppers, 1 tsp oregano, dill sprigs, salt.

Cut the tops off the onions, and make the edges jagged. Put into a pot, cover with sour cream, and cook for 5-8 min. Then carefully remove the outer layers from the onions, leaving ever smaller bulbs.

Finely slice or mash the mushrooms, adding the egg, the pepper, chopped oregano, and remaining onion centers after finely chopping them. Add salt and mix thoroughly. Melt the butter in a frying pan, adding the mushroom mixture, and while stirring, sauté for 5 min.

Stuff the onion layers with the mushroom filling.

Set the onions up on a plate (the bigger ones in the center, the smaller ones on the sides; or as towers – with a bigger one on the bottom, 3-4 smaller ones on top). Pour the sour cream in which the onions were cooked over them, and sprinkle with chopped dill.

Serve with fried bread as a snack.

Onions Stuffed with Beets

Burokėliais įdaryti svogūnai

4 onions, 1 boiled pickled beet, 2-3 peppers, a pinch of sugar, 4 tbsps beet brine, salt.

Remove the insides from each onion, and finely chop the insides.

Finely dice the beet, adding the chopped onion, salt, and a pinch of sugar. Grind the pepper and add it, mixing thoroughly.

Put the beet mixture into the hollowed-out onion bulbs. Set the stuffed onions a plate, and pour the strained beet brine over them.

They can be served with hot boiled or baked potatoes, or other dishes.

Mixed Vegetables with Herring

Daržovių kratinys su silke

1 boiled pickled beet, 2 boiled potatoes, ½ cup boiled peas, ½ cup boiled, 1 pickle, 1 onion, 1 herring, 2 tbsps grated horseradish, 200 g sour cream, 1 tbsp dill seeds, dill sprigs, salt.

Finely dice the potatoes, pickle, and beet. Put into a bowl, adding a finely chopped onion and the deboned herring, cut into small pieces. Add the horseradish, peas, broad beans or garden beans the dill seeds (after washing with boiling water), sour cream, and salt. Mix thoroughly. Sprinkle chopped dill on top.

Vegetables with Smoked Cod

Daržovės su rūkyta menke

3 boiled potatoes, 1 cup boiled peas, 300 g smoked cod, 2 onions, 3 tbsps cooking oil, 1 pickle, 200 g sour cream, green onions, lovage leaves, salt.

Finely dice the potatoes and pickle. Finely chop the onions, and sauté in oil. When almost done, add chopped lovage leaves and sliced cod, and cook 2–3 more min.

Put the diced potatoes and pickle into a bowl, add the onions and cod, peas, sour cream, and salt, mixing thoroughly. Sprinkle with chopped green onions.

Vegetables with Fried Linseed

Daržovės su sėmenų spirgučiu

3 boiled potatoes, 1 boiled carrot, 2 cloves garlic, 2 tsps linseed, 3 tsps cooking oil, 1 onion, pepper, parsley leaves, salt.

Finely dice the carrot and potatoes. Fry the linseed in a frying pan, and mash or grind. Put the diced carrot and potatoes into a bowl, pour the finely chopped onion sautéed in oil over it. Add chopped parsley leaves, finely chopped garlic, ground pepper, and salt, mixing thoroughly. Sprinkle the fried linseed on top.

Vegetable Dumplings

Daržovių kukuliai

1 boiled carrot, 1 boiled rutabaga, 1 boiled parsley root, 1 boiled celery root, lovage leaves, 3 eggs, 3 tbsps bread crumbs, 2 onions, 2 tbsps butter, 300 g sour cream, dill sprigs, flour for rolling, cooking oil, salt.

Grind the boiled carrot, parsley, celery, and rutabaga in a meat grinder. Add the eggs, bread crumbs, finely chopped onions sautéed in butter, finely chopped lovage leaves, and salt, kneading everything together well. From this mixture make small dumplings (2–3 cm in diameter), roll in flour, and deep-fry in heated fat until golden brown (for 10-15 min.).

Remove the dumplings, put into a bowl, and pour over with sour cream. Sprinkle with chopped dill.

Vegetable and Mushroom Dumplings

Daržovių ir grybų kukuliai

1 cup boiled peas, 1 cup boiled garden beans, 3 boiled carrots, 1 cup bread crumbs, 2 eggs, 1 onion, 1 cup boiled mushrooms, 2 tbsps butter, 1 cup sour cream, ground pepper, parsley leaves, tarragon, flour for rolling, cooking oil, salt, 200 g sour cream.

Grind the boiled peas, garden beans, carrots, and mushrooms in a meat grinder. Add the eggs, crumbs, finely chopped onion sautéed in butter, finely chopped tarragon, pepper, and salt. Knead well. From this mixture make walnut-sized dumplings, roll in flour, and deep-fry in heated fat until golden brown (for 10–15 min.).

Remove the dumplings, put into a bowl, pouring sour cream over them, and sprinkle with chopped parsley leaves.

Celery Croquettes with Fish

Salierų maltiniai su žuvimi

600 g celery roots, 100 g bread,
300 g deboned fish, 2 eggs,
200 g butter, 1 tsp caraway seeds,
parsley leaves, cooking fat,
flour for rolling, salt.

Clean the celery, cut into thick slices, and boil in salted water for 10 min. Soak the bread in milk or water.

Remove the celery, drain off the water, and let cool. After squeezing out the liquid, grind the soaked bread together with the celery and fish with a meat grinder, adding the eggs, caraway seeds, and salt. Mix well. From this mixture make small croquettes, roll in flour, and fry in heated fat.

After frying, pour over with melted butter, sprinkle with chopped parsley leaves.

Serve with boiled potatoes and pickles or sauerkraut for lunch.

Black Salsify with Cheese

Gelteklės su sūriu

½ kg black salsify,
300 g farmer's cheese,
200 g butter,
tarragon, salt.

Clean the black salsify, and boil in salted water. When done, pour off the water, put into a baking pan, pour over with melted butter, and sprinkle with chopped tarragon and grated cheese. Put the pan into a slow to moderate oven, and heat for 5–10 min.

Serve this dish in the same pan in which it was baked.

Serve for dinner.

Squash Pancakes with Potatoes

Moliūgų blynai su bulvėmis

½ kg squash, ½ kg potatoes,
2 eggs, 4 tbsps flour,
1 onion, 200 g sour cream,
pepper, lemon balm,
cooking fat, salt.

Peel and finely grate the squash. Peel and wash the potatoes. Finely grate along with the onion. Put the grated squash and potatoes into a bowl, adding flour, egg yolks beaten with salt, ground pepper, and chopped lemon balm, mixing well. Beat the egg whites until stiff, and add to the gratings, mixing it in well.

In a frying pan, fry on both sides in heated fat.

Serve hot with sour cream.

Carrot Pancakes

Morkų blynai

1 l finely grated carrots,
2 eggs, 4 tbsps potato starch,
100 g sour cream, 5 tbsps sugar,
1 tsp lemon balm, salt,
butter or cooking oil.

Peel and finely grate the carrots, adding the starch, egg yolks, and salt. Mix well. Beat the egg whites, and add along with the chopped lemon balm leaves, mixing once more.

Spoon the carrot mixture into a frying pan with heated fat. Make small pancakes (the size of the amount in a tablespoon), and fry on both sides until golden brown.

Serve the pancakes hot with sour cream and sprinkled with sugar.

Kepti obuoliai ir kriaušės

3 sweet and sour apples, 3 pears,
3 tbsps ground cinnamon,
3 tbsps powdered sugar.

Baked Apples and Pears

Wash the apples and pears and put them in a frying pan, baking them in a hot oven until soft. As they finish baking, sprinkle cinnamon on them and bake a further 10 min. Take the apples and pears out, decorating them with powdered sugar.

Serve hot or cool with milk.

This dish is made at the end of summer or early fall for the afternoon or dinner.

Kepta obuolienė

10 tart apples, 100 g butter,
½ tsp cinnamon, 3 tbsps sugar.

Baked Apple Sauce

Peel and slice the apples, and put them into a baking pan with heated butter. Bake in a moderate oven until the apples are soft. Then sprinkle with sugar and cinnamon, and bake a little longer.

Serve baked apple sauce with pancakes, kugel, or other dishes, or eat with white bread. This dish goes well with sweet milk.

Obuolių sūris

5 kg apples, 1½ kg sugar,
½ tsp ground cinnamon.

Apple Cheese

Peel and slice the apples, sprinkle with sugar, and after mixing thoroughly, let stand for 48 hrs. so that a juice forms. Pour the juice into a wide-brimmed pot or bowl, and cook over a low flame until about half evaporates and it begins to thicken and the colour darkens. Then add about ¾ of the apples, and cook for about an hour, while constantly stirring until the required thickness is achieved (when a spoon is run from one end of the pot to the other, the bottom can be seen for a while, and there is no longer any liquid). Now add the remaining apples and cinnamon, and cook a little longer while constantly stirring (for about half an hour) until the mixture stops sticking to the walls of the pot. The apples added later remain light in colour, with the cheese becoming marbled.

When the mixture is done, immediately spoon into a damp cheesecloth bag, and press down for a couple of days. Then hang the cheese in a dry, well-ventilated place to dry out. Keep the dried cheese in a cold, dry place.

Apple cheese is a holiday food. Serve cut into slices or strips with tea, coffee, or wine.

potatoes

Steamed Potatoes in their Skins

Neskustos bulvės, virtos garuose

10 potatoes, 1 cup milk, 1 cup water, 1 tbsp caraway seeds, 1 tbsp fresh or dried dill, 2 cloves garlic, salt.

Pour the water and milk into a pot, add salt, caraway seeds, dill, and finely chopped garlic. Place a steamer basket on top so that it does not touch the liquid. On it, put the potatoes, washed clean but not peeled. Cover tightly, and cook for 30 min.

Serve the potatoes steamed in their skins with raw sauerkraut and oil or some other dressing, or along with other dishes.

Stewed Potatoes

Šutbulvės

10 medium-sized potatoes, 4 cloves garlic, 1 cup water, 25 g butter, 1 tbsp caraway seeds, salt.

Wash the unpeeled potatoes well, and cut into halves. Put the halves into a pot, adding water, butter, caraway seeds, and finely chopped garlic.

Cook in a covered pot over a low flame until the potatoes are tender.

Serve the potatoes with sour milk (in the Žemaitija region, people eat them with kastinys, or sour cream butter), or serve with other dishes.

Boiled Potatoes in their Skins

Neskustos virtos bulvės

1 kg potatoes, 1 tbsp caraway seeds, ½ tbsp sugar, ½ tsp salt, fresh or dried dill.

Wash the unpeeled potatoes well, put into boiling water, and add salt, sugar, dill, and caraway seeds, cooking them until they are tender.

After the potatoes are done, pour off the water, and keep them over the flame until they dry a bit.

Potatoes in their Skins Stuffed with Herring

Silke įdarytos neskustos bulvės

8 potatoes, 200 g ground or finely sliced herring, 2 onions, 100 g butter, ground pepper, lovage leaves, salt.

Wash the potatoes, but do not peel. Cut into halves lengthwise, hollowing out each half with a teaspoon.

To the ground herring, add onions sautéed in butter, adding salt if needed, along with pepper and chopped lovage leaves, mixing well. Add this filling to each potato half. Then put into a baking pan, and bake in an oven for 25–30 min.

Serve with melted butter or sour cream.

Potatoes Stuffed with Fish

Žuvimi įdarytos bulvės

*5 big potatoes, 200 g fish fillets,
2 onions, 100 g butter,
1 tsp oregano,
pepper, salt.*

Peel each potato, cut off one end, and hollow out the inside.

Cut the fish fillets into little pieces and the onions into thin slices.

Into each hollowed potato, put several dollops of butter and pieces of fish, pressing the sliced onions in between the fish pieces, adding oregano, pepper, and salt. Place a dollop of butter on top, and cover with the piece of potato that was cut off. Cut the other end of each potato so that they can stand up.

Bake these potatoes in an oven in a well-greased baking pan.

Serve hot with sauerkraut or sour milk.

Potatoes Stuffed with Mushrooms

Grybais įdarytos bulvės

*8 potatoes, 2 onions,
1 egg, ½ cup bread crumbs,
2 cups dried mushrooms, 50 g butter,
lemon-balm and parsley leaves,
pepper, 200 g sour cream,
salt, cooking oil.*

Soak and cook the mushrooms, grind up, adding finely chopped onions sautéed in fat. Add ground pepper, chopped lemon balm leaves, bread crumbs, the egg, and salt. Mix well.

Peel the potatoes, cutting both ends off each potato so that they can stand on end. From one end of the potato, hollow out the inside with a teaspoon, leaving thin walls. Put some of the mushroom filling inside, and cover with a piece that was cut off the potato. Put into a baking pan, and after basting with fat, bake in a moderate oven (180 °C) for 30 min.

When the potatoes are done, stand them up neatly on a platter, and pour the mushroom broth heated with sour cream over them. Sprinkle with parsley leaves.

Grated Potatoes (Kugel, Potato Pudding)

Bulvių tarkainis

*1 kg potatoes, 1 cup milk,
2 eggs, 2 onions,
1 tbsp chopped tarragon,
salt, fat.*

Peel the potatoes and grate finely, pouring off the liquid. Bring the milk to a boil, and pour over the grated potatoes, adding finely chopped onions sautéed in fat. Add the eggs, chopped tarragon, and salt, mixing well. Spoon this mixture into a greased baking pan or dish, and bake in an oven until the top turns golden brown.

When the grated potatoes are done, cut into little squares. Serve with a sauce of butter and sour cream. Some people also like to eat potato pudding with unsweetened apple sauce.

Grated Potatoes with Buckwheat

Grikių tarkainis

1 kg potatoes, 1 cup milk, 1 cup buckwheat flour, 2 eggs, 100 g butter, 2 onions, 1 tsp marjoram, salt.

Peel the potatoes and grate, pouring off the liquid. Pour boiling milk over them, mixing well. Then add the eggs, flour, marjoram, finely chopped onions sautéed in butter, and salt, again mixing well.

Put this mixture into a greased baking pan, making a layer 5–8 cm thick. Bake in a hot oven (220 °C) for about an hour.

When the grated potatoes are done, cut into oblong pieces.

Serve hot with melted butter or sour cream.

Grated Potatoes with Poppy Seeds or Hemp Seed

Tarkainis su aguonomis ar kanapėmis

1 kg potatoes, 1 cup poppy seeds or hemp seed, 2 onions, 200 g butter, 1 tbsp mint, salt.

Peel and grate the potatoes, pouring off the liquid, and adding onions sautéed in butter. Add salt, mint, and poppy seeds or hemp seed. Mix well.

Spoon this mixture into a greased baking pan, and bake in a moderate oven (180 °C) for about an hour.

When the grated potatoes are done, cut into oblong pieces. Serve hot with sour cream and butter sauce, with hemp seed or poppy seed milk, lingonberry preserves or apple sauce.

Grated Potatoes with Dried Mushrooms

Tarkainis su džiovintais grybais

1 kg potatoes, 100 g butter, 2 cups boiled finely sliced dried mushrooms, 2 eggs, 2 onions, 1 tsp oregano, pepper, salt.

Grate the potatoes, pouring off the liquid and adding chopped oregano, sliced mushrooms, and finely chopped onions sautéed in butter. Add salt. Mix everything, add the eggs, and again mix well.

Pour this mixture into a greased baking pan, and bake in an oven for about an hour.

When the grated potatoes are done, cut into small squares. Serve hot or warmed up with melted butter or sour cream.

Grated Potato Cold Noses

Tarkiniai šaltanosiai

1 l grated potatoes, 2 cups buckwheat flour, 1 cup hemp seed or poppy seeds, salt.

Add the flour and salt to the grated potatoes, and knead well. Roll this dough to a thickness of 1–2 cm, sprinkle with hemp seed or poppy seeds, and make into a roll. Put into a greased baking pan, and bake in an oven for about half an hour.

Serve cold noses cut into slices.

Grated Potatoes with Yeast

Mielinis tarkainis

1 kg potatoes, 30 g yeast,
½ cup milk, 100 g butter,
2 cups flour, 1 onion,
100 g cottage cheese,
1 tsp sugar, 1 tsp mint, salt.

Peel and grate the potatoes in the evening. Dissolve the yeast in luke warm sweetened milk, and let rise a bit. Then mix the grated potatoes, yeast, and flour, and keep overnight in a warm place so that the mixture becomes porous.

In the morning, spoon the mixture into a greased baking pan, and bake in a moderate oven (180 °C) for about an hour.

To make the sauce, finely chop the onion, and sauté in butter. To the sautéed onion, add mashed cottage cheese and chopped mint, mixing well.

Pour the sauce over the hot potato pudding after cutting into pieces.

Potato Dumplings

Didžkukuliai

1 kg raw potatoes,
4 boiled potatoes, salt.

Peel and grate the potatoes, squeezing them out through a double layer of cheesecloth. Do not dispose of the liquid, but wait until the starch has settled. Then pour off the liquid, and add the starch to the grated pota toes. Mash the boiled potatoes.

Thoroughly mix the grated potatoes and starch with the boiled potatoes, adding salt, and kneading well. Make pancakes that are not too thick, each from about 100 g of dough. Add a tablespoon of filling, press the edges firmly together, and make oblong dumplings. Put into boiling salted water, and cook for 30 min. while carefully stirring.

Potato dumplings are a fairly recent traditional food that became popular only in the middle of the last century. However, they spread very quickly and became a favorite dish throughout Lithuania. Potato dumplings are a very hearty food. Thus, hosts served them to those who helped with the farm work, and during the potato harvest they nourished the household.

Potato dumplings are made with various fillings:

Fish Filling

Žuvies įdaras

500 g pike, cod, flounder, zander, or some other fish, 2 onions, 3 tbsps bread crumbs, 50 g butter,1 tbsp sour cream, 1 egg, 1 tsp marjoram, pepper, salt.

Remove the bones from the fish, and grind the fillet, adding onions sautéed in butter, sour cream, bread crumbs, egg, seasonings, and salt. Knead well.

Serve the potato dumplings with fish filling with melted butter and sour cream, sauerkraut, or pickles.

Cottage Cheese Filling

Varškės įdaras

300 g cottage cheese, 1 egg,
1 tbsp sour cream, 50 g butter,
1 tsp tarragon or mint, salt.

Mash the cottage cheese, add the butter, sour cream, tarragon or mint, egg, and salt. Mix well.

Serve potato dumplings with cottage cheese filling with melted butter or sour cream.

Mushroom Filling

Grybų įdaras
½ l dried or salted mushrooms,
2 onions, 100 g butter, 1 egg,
2 tbsps bread crumbs,
1 tbsp oregano, salt.

If the mushrooms are dried, soak them for 2–3 hrs., and then cook in the same water. If they are salted, soak well, and cook in fresh water. Grind the cooked mushrooms with a meat grinder, adding chopped onions sautéed in butter, the egg, bread crumbs, chopped oregano, and salt. Mix well.

Serve potato dumplings with mushroom filling with melted butter or sour cream.

In the Dzūkija region, women make a special sauce for these dumplings. They sauté chopped onions in butter, add a teaspoon of flour, the mushroom broth and ground pepper, and bring the sauce to a boil.

Sauerkraut Filling

Raugintų kopūstų įdaras
1 l sauerkraut, 100 g butter,
2 onions.

Wash the sauerkraut, and add finely chopped onions sautéed in butter. Put the sauerkraut into a pot, and stew until tender.

Serve the potato dumplings with sauerkraut filling with melted butter or sour cream.

Herring Filling

Silkių įdaras
1 herring, 1 egg, 1 onion,
50 g butter, 2 tbsps bread crumbs,
1 tbsp lemon balm, pepper.

Soak the herring well, removing the bones and grinding the herring up or chopping very finely. Add a finely chopped onion sautéed in fat, along with the bread crumbs, ground pepper, chopped lemon balm, and egg. Mix well.

Serve potato dumplings with herring filling with sour cream, melted butter, or sauerkraut.

Žemaičių Potato Dumplings with Cottage Cheese and Poppy Seeds

Žemaitiški bulviniai
kukuliai su varške
ir aguonomis
FOR THE FILLING:
300 g cottage cheese,
3 tbsps poppy seeds,
1 tsp crushed mint,
1 egg, 50 g butter,
1 tbsp sour cream, salt.

Prepare the grated potato dough in the same way as for potato dumplings.

Mash the cottage cheese, adding the butter, sour cream, poppy seeds, mint, and salt. Mix well.

From this potato dough make pancakes the size of your palm, put cottage cheese filling on them, squeeze the edges together and make round dumplings. Put into boiling salted water, and cook for about 30 min. Sometimes these dumplings are made flat. In the Žemaitija region, people call them wheel dumplings (rateliniai kleckai).

Serve with melted butter and hemp seed or poppy seed milk.

Potato Pasties
with Hemp Seed Curd

**Bulviniai pyragiukai
su kanapių varške**

FOR THE FILLING:
½ l hemp seed, 1 l boiled water,
ground pepper, tarragon, salt.

Prepare the grated potato dough in the same way as for potato dumplings.

Toast the hemp seed for 3–5 min. in a frying pan, and while still hot, pour into a mortar and grind into a floury mixture. Pour the ground hemp seed into a bowl, add hot boiled water, and mix thoroughly. Pour into a cloth bag, and squeeze out. Add water, and squeeze out several more times.

Pour the resulting liquid into a pot, and slowly heat over a very low flame until it curdles. Pour off the liquid, add ground pepper, tarragon, and salt to the remaining curds, and mix well. From the potato dough, make pancakes the size of your palm, putting some hemp seed curd filling in the middle. Squeeze the edges together and make round dumplings. Put these dumplings into salted boiling water, and cook for 25–30 min.

Serve hot with melted butter and hemp seed or poppy seed milk.

Potatoes Stewed in Butter

Jušė

1 kg potatoes, 200 g butter,
1 tsp tarragon, dill sprigs, salt.

Peel and dice the potatoes, and put into a stewpot, adding ½ cup of water. Sprinkle with tarragon, and add butter and salt, stewing in an oven for 20–25 min.

Serve hot in the same pot in which they were baked, sprinkled with chopped dill.

Stewed Potatoes
and Mushrooms

Bulvių ir grybų šutinys

10 potatoes, 1 cup dried
mushrooms, 2 onions, 3 eggs,
100 g butter, 5 tbsps sour cream,
1 tbsp chopped oregano, salt.

Peel the potatoes and cut into slices. Put into boiling water, and cook for 3–5 min. Remove and drain.

Soak the dried mushrooms for 2 hrs., and then boil, cutting into strips. Slice the onions. In a greased pot, arrange in layers with the potatoes, onions, chopped hard-boiled eggs, mushrooms, and again with the same order until all the ingredients are used. Sprinkle with chopped oregano, add salt. The top layer must consist of potatoes. Pour over with sour cream mixed with mushroom broth.

Bake in a moderate oven (180 °C) for 30 min.

Serve these stewed potatoes in the same pot, poured over with melted butter. Serve for lunch with sauerkraut or pickles.

Stewed Potatoes, Mushrooms, and Sauerkraut

Bulvių, grybų
ir kopūstų šutinys

*½ kg potatoes, ½ l sauerkraut,
1 cup fresh or salted mushrooms,
2 onions, 100 g butter,
100 g sour cream, oregano, salt.*

Soak the mushrooms well if they are salted, or partially cook if they are fresh. Wash the sauerkraut if it is very sour.

Into a greased pan, put half of the peeled potatoes cut into eighths, and sprinkle with salt. Put a layer of sauerkraut on top, pouring melted butter over it. On the sauerkraut, put sliced mushrooms, sprinkle with chopped oregano, and cover with onion slices. Put the remaining potatoes on top, add salt, and pour the sour cream over it. Bake in a moderate oven (180 °C) for 40–45 min.

Serve this potato dish hot for lunch.

Stewed Potatoes, Herring, and Sauerkraut

Bulvių, silkių
ir kopūstų šutinys

*½ kg potatoes, ½ l sauerkraut,
2 herrings, 2 onions,
100 g butter, 100 g sour cream,
2 tbsps caraway seeds,
lovage leaves, salt.*

Peel and dice the potatoes. Peel the herring, remove the bones, and slice into strips. Wash the sauerkraut if it is very sour, adding the sliced herring, finely chopped onions sautéed in butter, chopped lovage leaves, and salt, mixing thoroughly.

In a greased pot, arrange a layer of diced potatoes, and sprinkle with caraway seeds and salt. Put the sauerkraut on top of the potatoes, then add the rest of the potatoes. Sprinkle with caraway seeds, add salt, and pour the sour cream over it. Bake in a moderate oven (180 °C) for 30–35 min.

Stewed Potatoes and Fish in Mushroom Sauce

Bulvių ir žuvų
šutinys grybų padaže

*10 potatoes, ½ kg fresh fish,
1 egg, 1 onion, 50 g butter,
pepper, 2 tsps marjoram, 5 dried
mushrooms, ½ cup sour cream,
1 tbsp bread crumbs, salt.*

Peel the potatoes, cut into thin slices, and put into salted boiling water, cooking for 5 min. Remove and drain. Cut the fish into small pieces, adding a sautéed onion, butter, egg, marjoram, pepper, and salt. Mix well.

Soak the mushrooms for 2 hrs., and cook in a small amount of water. When they are done, cut into strips and put into the broth in which they were cooked. Put half of the partially cooked potatoes into a greased pot. On top, put the fish mixture and then the remaining potatoes, pouring the mushroom sauce over it. Sprinkle with bread crumbs, and bake in an oven for 15–20 min.

Serve with sauerkraut or pickles for lunch.

Bulvių ir silkių šutinys

1 kg potatoes, 3 herrings, 2 onions, 300 g sour cream, 50 g butter, pepper, 3 tbsps finely grated horseradish, 1 tsp sugar, salt.

Stewed Potatoes and Herring

Peel the potatoes, and cut into thin slices. Soak the herring, peel, remove the bones, and cut into pieces 2 cm in size. In a greased pot, arrange a layer of potatoes, sprinkle with ground pepper and finely chopped onions, pouring melted butter over it. On top of the potatoes arrange a layer of herring, then of potatoes again, and keep repeating until everything is used up. The top layer should consist of the potatoes. Over this top layer, pour 100 g of sour cream. Bake in a moderate oven (180 °C) for 20–25 min.

Serve these potatoes hot in the same pot in which they were baked.

Serve with horseradish sauce. To make the sauce, mix the horseradish with 200 g sour cream, add 1 tsp sugar, salt, and mix well.

Troškė

10 potatoes, 1 cup sour cream, 1 cup buttermilk, green onions, dill, parsley leaves, marjoram, salt.

Stewed Potatoes

Peel the potatoes. Cook them in salted water, and pour off the water. Pour the buttermilk and sour cream into a bowl, add salt, chopped green onions, dill, parsley, and marjoram, mixing thoroughly. Pour this sauce over the hot boiled potatoes, and heat for 2–3 min. over a low flame.

This is a popular dish in the Suvalkija region, where people make it for lunch. They eat it with cold beet soup, sour milk, or pickles. It is an especially delicious dish when fresh potatoes are used.

Kiunkė

3 medium-sized potatoes, ½ l peas, 100 g butter, 2 onions, 1 tsp chopped sage, salt.

Potatoes with Peas

Soak the peas, and cook until tender. In another pot, cook the potatoes after peeling and cutting them into pieces. When the potatoes are almost done, add the peas, and cook for 5 min more. Then pour off the water and mash everything, adding salt.

Add finely chopped onions and sage to heated butter and sauté.

Spoon the mashed potatoes into a bowl, making a small indentation in the middle where the sautéed onions can be placed.

In the Žemaitija region, people eat potatoes with peas for breakfast with sauerkraut, and with sour milk in the summer months.

Potatoes with Broad Beans

Kiunkė su pupomis

*½ l broad beans,
4 medium-sized potatoes,
1 tbsp dill seed, salt, water.*

Soak the broad beans well and cook. Peel the potatoes, cut into pieces, and cook in a small amount of water with the dill seed. When the potatoes are done, pour off the water, add the beans, and mash everything together, adding salt.

Serve for breakfast with sour milk, cheese, pickles, or sauerkraut. On hot days this dish goes well with beer.

Potatoes with Sauerkraut

Kiunkė su kopūstais

*½ kg potatoes, ½ kg sauerkraut,
100 g cooking oil or butter,
3 juniper berries, 1 onion, salt.*

Peel the potatoes, cut into pieces, and put into boiling water. Do not use much water. When the potatoes are tender, add the sauerkraut, and sprinkle with crushed juniper berries. Add salt. Cook for 15 min. more. Pour off the water and shake well in the pot.

Finely dice the onions, sauté in fat, and pour over the potatoes and sauerkraut, shaking the mixture once more.

This kind of potato dish is also called hodgepodge (kratinys).

Baked Mashed Potatoes with Mushrooms

Virtų bulvių apkepas su grybais

*10 potatoes, ½ l milk,
1 egg, 1 onion, 150 g butter,
1 cup boiled fresh or dried
mushrooms, 1 tbsp bread
crumbs, 1 tbsp chopped
oregano, salt.*

Peel and boil the potatoes, pour off the water, and mash, adding hot milk and salt. Mix well.

Finely chop the onion and sauté in butter. Add finely chopped mushrooms and fry briefly, adding the bread crumbs and oregano. Heat a little longer.

In a greased pan arrange a layer of mashed potatoes, a layer of sautéed mushrooms, and another layer of mashed potatoes. On top pour a beaten egg, add the remaining butter, and bake in a slow oven (160 °C) for 25 min.

Serve this dish hot with sour milk.

Baked Potatoes with Sauerkraut

Bulvių apkepas su raugintais kopūstais

*10 potatoes, 100 g butter,
1 cup sauerkraut, 2 onions,
1 tbsp dill seed, pepper, salt.*

Boil the potatoes in their skins, peel, and cut into thick slices. Put the sliced potatoes into a greased pot, sprinkle with dill seed, and add finely chopped onions sautéed in butter. Put the sauerkraut on top. Cover and stew over a low flame for 10–15 min.

Serve with sour milk for lunch or in the afternoon.

Baked Mashed Potatoes with Cabbage

**Bulvių apkepas
su kopūstais**

*10 potatoes, ½ l milk,
½ l fresh cabbage, 1 egg,
1 tsp caraway seeds, 2 onions,
150 g butter, lovage leaves, salt.*

Peel and boil the potatoes. Pouring off the water, mash the potatoes, adding hot milk, salt, and caraway seeds. Mix well. Cut a head of cabbage into several parts, and partially cook in well-salted water.

In a greased pan, arrange a layer of mashed potatoes, a layer of chopped cabbage mixed with sautéed onions and lovage leaves, and again mashed potatoes. On top pour an egg beaten with 2 tbsps of milk and a pinch of salt, add dollops of butter, and bake in an oven for 25–30 min.

Serve this baked dish hot for lunch with salad or fresh cucumbers.

Baked Potatoes with Herring

Bulvių ir silkių apkepas

*10 potatoes, 3 herrings, 2 onions,
1 egg, 50 g butter, 20 g cooking oil,
2 tbsps bread crumbs, parsley leaves,
1 tsp lemon balm leaves.*

Boil the potatoes in their skins, peel, and slice. Soak the herring, removing the bones and cutting into small pieces. Chop the onion, sauté in oil, and mix with the herring. Add the lemon balm. In a greased pan arrange layers of potatoes first, and then herring, repeating this until the ingredients run out. Put the butter on top, sprinkle with chopped parsley leaves, pouring the beaten egg over it. Sprinkle with bread crumbs.

Bake in a slow oven (160 °C) for 15 min.

Serve for lunch with pickled beets or pickles.

Potato Roll with Sauerkraut and Mushrooms

**Bulvių vyniotinis su
kopūstais ir grybais**

*1 l mashed boiled potatoes, 3 eggs,
4 tbsps starch, ½ l sauerkraut,
½ cup cooking oil, 2 onions,
1 cup boiled and ground dried
mushrooms, 200 g butter,
lovage leaves, salt.*

Add the eggs to the potatoes, adding starch and salt, and kneading thoroughly.

Stew the sauerkraut with oil, add finely chopped sautéed onions, the mushrooms, and chopped lovage leaves. Mix thoroughly and stew.

From the potato dough make a large pancake the thickness of your finger. Spread the stewed sauerkraut with mushrooms over it, and make a roll. Put the roll into a greased baking pan, and spread the beaten egg over it. Bake in a moderate oven (180 °C) for 15–20 min. When the roll is done, cut into slices.

Serve hot with melted butter.

Half-and-Half Porridge

Pusmarškonė košė

1 kg small potatoes, 1 cup rye flour,
½ l milk, 100 g butter,
2 onions, 3 tbsps sour cream,
2 tbsps caraway seeds, salt.

Wash the small potatoes well, removing their eyes. Boil the potatoes in their skins. When the potatoes are done, pour off the water and mash. Pour the water back in which they were boiled, mix thoroughly, and press through a sieve. Add the milk to this mixture. Pour the resulting purée into a pot and heat. When it begins to boil, gradually add the flour while stirring, adding salt and caraway seeds, and cook while constantly stirring for 5 min. more.

When the porridge is done, spoon into a bowl, making a small indentation in the middle where the sauce can be put.

To make the sauce, finely dice the onions and put into a frying pan, and sauté in butter over a low flame. Before the onions are done, add the sour cream.

Serve hot with sour milk.

Potato Porridge

Marškonė košė

1 kg potatoes, ½ l milk or cream,
1 tsp chopped tarragon,
salt, 50 g butter.

Peel the potatoes and put them into a pot, adding cold water, and boil until they begin to crack. Then pour off the water, and mash in the pot in which they were boiled. Pour milk or cream over the well-mashed potatoes, adding tarragon and salt, mix well, and while constantly mixing, cook for 3–5 min. more.

When the porridge is done, spoon into a bowl, making a small indentation into which melted butter can be poured. Potato porridge made this way is light and tasty, but it quickly cools and hardens, so eat it hot as soon as it is done.

Serve with sweet or sour milk.

Mashed Potatoes with Seeds

Grūdielius

10 potatoes, ½ cup hemp seed
or poppy seeds, salt.

Peel the potatoes, adding water and salt. Boil until tender. When the potatoes are done, remove from the flame, pour off the water and mash, adding the poppy seeds or hemp seed, and mixing well. If the mashed potatoes are very thick, add some of the liquid in which they were boiled or some milk.

Serve in the afternoon or for supper with sour milk.

Lenten Fat

Gavėnios taukai

1 kg potatoes, 1 cup sour milk,
2 tbsps caraway seeds, salt.

Peel the potatoes. Add water, caraway seeds, and salt, boiling until tender. When the potatoes are done, pour off the water and mash, adding the sour milk. Mix well.

Serve hot with sour milk.

Dry Mashed Potatoes

Sausienė

*1 kg potatoes, 3 onions,
100 g butter, salt.*

Peel the potatoes, cuting each into four parts. Put into a pot, add water, and boil until tender. Then partially mash in the pot with a masher or a spoon, adding chopped onions sautéed in butter. Add butter and mix thoroughly.

Serve with sour or sweet milk. This dish is especially delicious when made from fresh potatoes.

Mashed Potatoes with Cottage Cheese

Bulvių košė su varške

*10 potatoes, 300 g cottage cheese,
50 g butter, mint leaves, salt.*

Peel the potatoes, adding water and salt. Boil until tender. When the potatoes are done, pour off the water and mash.

Mash the cottage cheese with butter, adding chopped mint, and mix thoroughly. Add the cottage cheese to the hot, freshly mashed potatoes, and mix well. If the mashed potatoes mixture is too thick, add a little milk or potato broth.

Serve hot with milk for supper or in the afternoon.

Mashed Potatoes with Mushrooms

Bulvių košė su grybais

*10 potatoes, 200 g mushrooms
(fresh, salted, or boiled dried),
100 g butter, 1 tsp marjoram,
1 onion, ground pepper,
100 g sour cream.*

Peel the potatoes, cutting into pieces and putting into boiling salted water. Cook until tender. When the potatoes are done, pour off the water and mash.

Boil the mushrooms, cuting into thin strips, and adding to finely chopped onions sautéed in butter, along with marjoram, and stew. To the stewed mushrooms, add the mashed potatoes, ground pepper, and sour cream, mixing well.

Serve these mashed potatoes hot in the afternoon or for dinner with milk.

Potatoes and Mushroom Croquettes

Bulvių ir grybų maltinukai

*1 l boiled mashed potatoes,
1 cup boiled fresh or salted
mushrooms, 2 eggs,
5 tbsps flour, 1 tbsp oregano,
salt, cooking fat.*

To the mashed potatoes, add ground or chopped mushrooms, eggs, flour, chopped oregano, and salt, kneading well. From this dough make croquettes, and fry in heated fat until both sides are browned.

Serve hot with melted sour cream heated in mushroom broth, melted butter, or sautéed onion and butter sauce.

Bulvių maltiniai su grybų padažu

10 potatoes, 2 eggs,
5 tbsps flour, 1 tbsp sour cream,
cooking fat, salt.
FOR THE SAUCE:
1 cup boiled dried mushrooms,
1 tbsp flour, 50 g butter,
1 cup mushroom broth,
1 onion, 1 tsp oregano, salt.

Potato Croquettes with Mushroom Sauce

Boil the potatoes, grinding them with a meat grinder or mash well. Add the flour, eggs, sour cream, and salt, kneading well. From this potato dough make little croquettes, rolling them in flour and frying them on both sides in heated fat.

To make the sauce, wash the mushrooms, and soak in water for 2–3 hrs. Then boil in the same water.

Fry the flour in butter, thinning it out with hot mushroom broth, and heat briefly, adding chopped oregano and finely chopped onion sautéed in butter, the mushrooms cut into strips, and salt. Mix thoroughly, and fry a little longer.

Serve hot for lunch.

Bulvių maltiniai su varškės įdaru

½ l boiled and mashed potatoes,
2 eggs, 1 tbsp starch,
200 g cottage cheese,
1 tsp marjoram, 100 g butter,
100 g sour cream, 3 tbsps flour,
salt, cooking fat.

Potato Turnovers with Cottage Cheese Filling

Add an egg to the mashed potatoes, along with starch and salt, and knead.

Mash the cottage cheese, adding an egg, the marjoram, and salt. Knead the mixture.

From the potato dough make round pancakes, and in the middle of each put some of the cottage cheese filling. Fold in half, and firmly squeeze the edges together. Roll these turnovers in flour, and fry in fat in a frying pan, frying on both sides until golden brown.

Serve these pancakes for breakfast or lunch with melted butter or sour cream.

In the Žemaitija region, homemakers serve sour cream butter (kastinys) with these pancakes.

Bulviniai pyragėliai su varške

10 potatoes, 3 eggs, 2 tbsps flour,
1 onion, 200 g cottage cheese,
1 tbsp mint, salt, cooking fat.

Potato Rolls with Cottage Cheese

Boil the potatoes, grind with a meat grinder or mash. To the mashed potatoes add a finely chopped onion, flour, a beaten egg, and salt, kneading well. From this potato dough make pancakes. Put some well-mashed cottage cheese mixed with mint on each of them, and make oblong rolls.

Put these rolls into hot fat, and deep-fry until golden brown.

Serve these rolls with tea.

Baked Potato Pasties "Wooden Spoons"

Kepti bulviniai
pyragėliai "kukoriai"

10 potatoes,
3 tbsps flour, salt.

Boil the potatoes in their skins and peel them. Grind with a meat grinder, and add flour and salt. From the potato dough roll pancakes about 8–10 cm in diameter. Put some filling on each of them, firmly squeezing the edges together. Put the wooden spoons into a greased baking pan, and bake in a moderate oven (180 °C) until golden brown (for 20–25 min.).

Wooden spoons can be made with various fillings:

Carrot Filling

Morkų įdaras

3 boiled carrots,
1 onion, 50 g butter,
1 tbsp lemon balm, salt.

Cook the carrots, peel, and coarsely grate. Chop the onion, sauté in butter, adding chopped lemon balm and salt, and mixing everything thoroughly.

Serve wooden spoons with carrot filling for breakfast or lunch with melted butter or sour cream.

Sauerkraut Filling

Kopūstų įdaras

1 cup sauerkraut, 50 g butter,
1 tbsp dill seeds, 1 onion, salt.

Finely chop the onion, and sauté in butter. Then add the sauerkraut, dill seeds, and stew for 10 min.

Serve wooden spoons with sauerkraut along with warmed sour cream poured over the top.

Mushroom Filling

Grybų įdaras

1 cup boiled salted or dried
mushrooms, 1 onion,
50 g butter, 1 egg,
2 tbsps bread crumbs,
1 tsp oregano, salt.

Finely chop the onion, and sauté in butter. To the sautéed onion add finely chopped or ground boiled mushrooms, chopped oregano, the egg, bread crumbs, and salt, mixing well.

Serve wooden spoons with mushrooms for lunch with butter and sour cream sauce.

Cottage Cheese Filling

Varškės įdaras

200 g cottage cheese,
1 tbsp mint, salt.

Add salt and mint to the cottage cheese, and mash well.

Serve wooden spoons filled with cottage cheese with sweet milk or mint tea.

Groat Filling

Kruopų įdaras

1 cup fine barley groats,
50 g butter, 1 onion,
1 tbsp oregano, salt.

Pour boiling water over the groats, cover, and let stand for about an hour so that they swell up. Chop the onion, sauté in butter, and add this to the groats, along with chopped oregano and salt. Mix thoroughly.

Serve wooden spoons with groat filling along with melted butter or sour cream poured over the top.

Švilpikai

10 potatoes, 1 cup flour,
3 eggs, 100 g butter,
3 tbsps sour cream, salt.
FOR THE SAUCE:
100 g cottage cheese,
½ cup milk, green onions,
dill sprigs, salt.

Marmots

Boil the potatoes in their skins and peel them. Mash the potatoes, adding the flour, 2 eggs, and salt. Knead the mixture. Form a roll out of the potato dough, flatten, and cut diagonally into little diamond shapes. Put into a baking pan sprinkled with flour, spreading the beaten egg on it, and bake in a not very hot oven (180 °C) for 10–15 min.

When the marmots are done, put into a dish, pouring melted butter and sour cream over them. Stew for 10 min. in a warm oven.

In the Aukštaitija region, people call this dish potato squares (bulbonai) and eat it with cottage cheese sauce. To make the sauce, mash the cottage cheese while gradually adding milk. Also add finely chopped green onions, dill, and salt, mixing thoroughly.

Serve hot.

Bulvių riestainiukai su žuvimi

10 potatoes, 100 g boiled ground
fish, 3 tbsps starch, 2 eggs,
50 g butter, ½ cup sour cream,
1 onion, marjoram, tarragon,
pepper, celery leaves,
salt, cooking fat.

Potato Rings with Fish

Peel the potatoes and boil them in a small amount of water. Pour off the liquid and mash. To the mashed potatoes add the starch, chopped tarragon, 1 egg, and salt, kneading well.

To the ground fish add a finely chopped onion sautéed in butter, marjoram, pepper, and eggs. Mix everything thoroughly, and fry briefly.

From the potato dough make little rings, and deep-fry in heated fat. When they are done, arrange on a plate, putting some of the ground fish in the middle of each ring.

Briefly cook the remaining butter with the sour cream, adding salt, and pour over the hot rings. Sprinkle with chopped celery leaves.

Bulvių riestainiukai su varške

10 potatoes, 100 g cottage cheese,
3 tbsps starch, 2 eggs, 50 g butter,
2 tbsps sour cream, 1 tbsp mint,
salt, cooking fat.

Potato Rings with Cottage Cheese

Peel the potatoes and boil them in a small amount of water. Pour off the liquid, and mash, adding the starch, 1 egg, and salt. Knead well.

Mash the cottage cheese well, adding the sour cream, 1 egg, and finely chopped mint. Mix thoroughly, and sauté in butter.

From the potato dough make little rings, and deep-fry in hot fat. When they are done, arrange them on a plate, putting some of the cottage cheese in the middle of each.

Before serving, pour melted butter over the hot rings.

Serve with mint or some other herbal tea.

Bulvių kukuliai grybų padaže

1 kg potatoes, 1 onion, 1 tbsp butter, dill or parsley leaves,1 cup flour, 2 eggs, ½ cup bread crumbs, salt.
FOR THE SAUCE:
100 g butter, 1 cup boiled fresh or dried mushrooms, 1 onion, 4 tbsps sour cream, salt.

Potato Dumplings in Mushroom Sauce

Boil the potatoes in their skins. Peel the potatoes and mash. To the mashed potatoes add the flour, a finely chopped sautéed onion, the bread crumbs, finely chopped parsley or dill leaves, the eggs, and salt, kneading well.

From the potato dough make walnut-sized dumplings, and put into boiling salted water, cooking until they rise to the surface of the water. When the dumplings are done, put into a bowl, and pour over with mushroom sauce.

To make the sauce, boil the dried or fresh mushrooms, and slice into strips. Sauté a finely chopped onion in butter, adding the mushrooms and salt. Sauté a little longer, adding the sour cream and mixing thoroughly, pouring this sauce over the dumplings.

Serve hot.

Bulvių kukuliai su aguonomis

10 potatoes, 3 eggs, 3 tbsps starch, ½ cup poppy seeds, dill sprigs, salt, 100 g butter, 100 g sour cream.

Potato Dumplings with Poppy Seeds

Boil the potatoes in their skins, peel and mash. After the mashed potatoes have cooled, add the eggs, starch, dry poppy seeds, and salt, kneading the mixture well.

From this dough make little dumplings, putting them into salted boiling water, and cook until they rise to the surface of the water (for about 10 min.). When the dumplings are done, remove, drain, and pour over with butter heated with sour cream. Sprinkle with chopped dill.

Serve hot with sweet or sour milk.

Grūstiniai blynai su grybais

4–5 medium-sized boiled potatoes, 3 eggs, 3 tbsps flour, ½ cup boiled fresh or dried mushrooms, 1 onion,1 tsp marjoram, 1 tbsp butter, salt, cooking fat.

Mashed Potato Pancakes with Mushrooms

Mash the potatoes, adding the flour, eggs, finely chopped mushrooms, and chopped onion sautéed in butter, chopped marjoram, and salt. Mix well. Put spoonfuls of the resulting thick, fluffy batter into a frying pan with heated fat, and fry on both sides until the pancakes start to turn golden brown.

Serve hot with sauce made from sour cream dissolved in mushroom broth.

Potato Pancakes

Tarkiniai blynai

*1 kg potatoes, 2 eggs,
salt, cooking fat.*

Peel and wash the potatoes and grate finely, adding the eggs and salt, mixing thoroughly. Fry in heated fat until both sides are golden brown.

Serve with sour cream for breakfast or lunch. In the Aukštaitija region, people eat these pancakes with cottage cheese mashed in sour cream.

Potato Pancakes with Cottage Cheese

Tarkiniai blynai su varške

*1 l grated potatoes, 3 eggs,
200 g cottage cheese,
½ cup flour, 1 tbsp mint,
salt, cooking fat.*

Spoon the grated potatoes into mashed cottage cheese, adding the eggs, flour, chopped mint, and salt. Mix well.

Put this batter, one tablespoon at a time, into a frying pan with heated fat. Fry on both sides until golden brown.

Serve these pancakes with sour cream, sugar, apple sauce, or various berry preserves.

Potato Pancakes Baked on Cabbage Leaves

Tarkiniai blynai, kepti ant kopūstų lapų

*8 raw potatoes, 3 boiled potatoes,
100 g butter, 3 tbsps sour cream,
1 tsp tarragon, cabbage leaves, salt.*

Peel and grate the potatoes, pouring off some of the liquid. Add salt, mashed boiled potatoes, and chopped tarragon, mixing thoroughly. On each clean cabbage leaf put 3 tablespoons of batter, flatten, and bake in an oven until golden brown.

After removing, peel off the cabbage leaves, and put the pancakes into a dish one on top of the other, pouring melted butter, sour cream, or poppy seed milk over them, and heat for a few more minutes until they are softer.

In the Žemaitija region, people bake these pancakes during the potato harvest. They bake them in the morning, pour sour cream over them, and leave them in the oven. They are usually eaten for lunch.

In the Aukštaitija and the Dzūkija regions, people call these pancakes loaves (bandos). They eat them for breakfast with sour cream or cottage cheese mashed in sour cream. Loaves are also eaten with honey spread over them and heated.

Potato Pancakes with Poppy Seeds

Tarkiniai blynai su aguonomis

1 l grated potatoes, 1 cup poppy seeds, ½ cup flour, 2 eggs, 3 allspice berries, 1 tsp lemon balm, salt, cooking fat.

To the grated potatoes, add the dry clean poppy seeds, flour, ground allspice, chopped lemon balm, eggs, and salt, mixing well. Fry in heated fat.

Serve these pancakes with melted butter or thick sour cream whipped with sugar.

Grated and Boiled Potatoes Pancakes

Tarkiniai blynai su virtomis bulvėmis

8 raw potatoes, 3 boiled potatoes,1 egg, 2 tbsps flour, 1 cup sour milk, 1 tsp tarragon, salt, cooking fat.

Peel and grate the potatoes. Squeezing out the grated potatoes, grind or mash the boiled potatoes, adding the flour, chopped tarragon, egg, sour milk, and salt. Mix well.

Fry in heated fat by spooning in one tablespoon at a time of this batter.

In the Aukštaitija region, people eat these pancakes with sour cream or with cottage cheese mashed with sour cream.

Cottage Cheese Buns with Grated Potatoes

Kepti tarkiniai varškėčiai

8 potatoes, 200 g cottage cheese, 100 g butter, 2 eggs, 2 tbsps sour cream, 1 tbsp mint, salt.

Peel and grate the potatoes, pouring off the liquid. To the grated potatoes add mashed cottage cheese, crushed mint, an egg, and salt, kneading well. Make small buns and put into a greased baking pan, spreading beaten egg on them, and bake in a moderate oven (180 °C) until golden brown. When done, put the buns into a bowl, pour hot sour cream and butter sauce over them, and cover, heating them in the oven for 10 min.

Serve hot in the afternoon or for dinner.

Potato Pancakes with Yeast

Tarkiniai blynai su mielėmis

1 kg potatoes, 25 g yeast, ½ cup sour milk, 1 cup flour, sugar, 1 tsp crushed tarragon, salt, cooking fat.

Dissolve the yeast in lukewarm milk, adding sugar, and let rise a bit. Grate the potatoes. Mix the grated potatoes with the sour milk and flour, adding yeast, chopped tarragon, and salt. Leave for an hour to rise.

Fry in heated fat by spooning in one tablespoon at a time of this batter.

Serve these pancakes hot with sour cream and butter sauce, cottage cheese sauce, baked apple sauce, or lingonberry preserves.

Potato Pancakes with Buckwheat Flour

Tarkiniai blynai su grikių miltais

1 kg potatoes, 1 egg, 1 cup buckwheat flour, 1 tsp thyme, salt, cooking fat.

Peel and finely grate the potatoes, adding the egg, flour, chopped thyme, and salt, mixing well.

Fry by putting one tablespoon at a time of this batter into heated fat. Brown both sides nicely.

Serve these pancakes hot with sour cream or with mashed cottage cheese, with sweet milk or cream poured over them.

This is a breakfast food in eastern Lithuania and the Dzūkija region.

Potato Buns

Tarkinės bandelės

8 potatoes, ½ l sour milk, 4 cups flour, 1 tsp tarragon, salt.

Peel and grate the potatoes, add the sour milk and a cup of flour. Mix thoroughly. Keep warm overnight. The next day add the remaining flour, chopped tarragon, and salt, kneading well.

Make buns, and bake in an oven in a greased baking pan until golden brown.

Serve hot with melted butter and sour cream for lunch.

Potato Bowls

Tarkiniai dubenėliai

8 raw potatoes, 5 boiled potatoes, salt.

Grate the potatoes. Squeeze out the grated potaotes, adding mashed boiled potatoes and salt, kneading well. From this dough make medium-sized dumplings, flattening each of them, and making a small indentation in each one. Put these little bowls into boiling salted water. Cook for 15–20 min.

Remove the bowls, and put into a dish with the indentations facing upward, pour onions sautéed in butter or with melted butter and sour cream over them.

In the Aukštaitija region, they are made in the shape of a pancake and are also called pancakes (blyneliai). In the Žemaitija region, these pancakes are sometimes also called fools (durniai).

Potato Dumplings

Tarkiniai kukuliai

1 l grated potatoes, ½ cup farina, 2 eggs, 1 cup milk, 1 tbsp starch, 1 tbsp mint, salt.

Cook the farina in milk. Let cool. Add to it the grated potatoes, eggs, salt, finely chopped mint leaves, and starch. Knead everything together well. Make small dumplings. Put into boiling salted water, and cook for 10–15 min.

After removing, pour butter or sour cream sauce over the dumplings.

Serve hot.

Potato Porridge

Tarkienė

1 kg potatoes, 300 g milk, 1 cup water, 1 tsp tarragon, salt, 200 g sour cream.

Peel and grate the potatoes. Pouring the water into a pot, and heat it until boiling. Before the water starts boiling, add the milk, and while continuing to heat and constantly stirring, add the grated potatoes, chopped tarragon, and salt. Cook while stirring until the grated potatoes no longer crunch between your teeth (for 10–15 min.).

When the porridge is done, spoon into a bowl, making a small indentation in the middle into which the sour cream can be poured.

Potato Porridge with Buckwheat

Tarkienė su grikiais

½ l grated potatoes, ½ l buckwheat groats, 1½ l water, 2 onions, 200 g butter, 1 tsp tarragon, salt.

Soak the buckwheat. Pour into a pot, add cold water, and cook while occasionally stirring. When the groats become tender, add salt and chopped tarragon. While constantly stirring, add the grated potatoes, and cook for another 10–15 min. (until the grated potatoes no longer crunch between your teeth).

Spoon the porridge into a bowl, making a small indentation in the middle into which the onions sautéed in butter can be poured. Serve hot with sweet or sour milk.

Potato Porridge with Caraway Seeds

Tarkienė su kmynais

½ l grated potatoes, 1 cup rye flour, 2 tbsps caraway seeds, 2 onions, 100 g butter, 50 g sour cream, 1 l water, salt.

Pour the caraway seeds into the water, and bring to a boil. Then, while stirring, add the grated potatoes, and cook for 5 min. Then add the flour and salt, and while constantly stirring, cook for 10 min.

When the porridge is done, spoon it into a bowl, making a small indentation in the middle to pour the finely chopped onions sautéed in butter and sour cream into.

Serve hot with sweet or sour milk.

Potatoes Baked with Cheese

Bulvės, apkeptos sūriu

10 potatoes, 3 eggs, 1 cup milk, 200 g dried farmer's cheese, 1 tbsp caraway seeds, 1 tbsp butter, mint leaves, salt.

Peel the potatoes and cut into thin slices, putting them into a baking pan greased with butter. Beat the eggs well, adding finely grated cheese, caraway seeds, chopped mint, milk, and salt. Mix thoroughly, and pour over the potatoes. Bake in a moderate oven until the top turns golden brown (for 20–25 min.).

Serve hot with milk or buttermilk and fresh or pickled vegetables.

Keptos bulvės su sūriu

*12 uniformly small potatoes,
100 g butter, 200 g sour cream,
200 g dried farmer's cheese,
dill sprigs, salt.*

Baked Potatoes with Cheese

Peel the potatoes, making several horizontal slits in each (do not make the slits to the end of the potato). Put the potatoes into a greased baking pan with their slits facing upward. Put butter into the slits, and on top sprinkle salt and finely grated cheese. Bake in a moderate oven (180 °C) for about 20 min. until the potatoes are tender and turn a beautiful golden colour. When the potatoes are done, put into a dish, and pour over with warmed sour cream. Sprinkle with plenty of chopped dill.

Serve these potatoes with fresh or pickled vegetables, or serve with other dishes.

Išrūgose šutintos bulvės

*1 kg potatoes, 1 cup whey,
1 onion, 50 g butter, 1 tbsp
dill seeds, dill sprigs, salt.*

Potatoes Stewed in Whey

Peel the potatoes and cut them into large pieces. Put the pieces into a pot, and sprinkle with finely chopped onion, dill seeds, and salt. Add the whey and stew. When the potatoes are almost done, add the butter.

Serve these potatoes in the same pot in which they were cooked sprinkled with chopped dill.

Serve hot with sour milk and fresh or pickled vegetables.

Bulvės su kanapėmis

*10 potatoes, 1 cup hemp seed,
1 onion, ground pepper,
salt, 2 tbsps cooking oil.*

Potatoes with Hemp Seed

Peel the potatoes, wash, and cook in a small amount of salted water. Pour off the water, and shake vigorously.

Pour clean hemp seed into a hot frying pan, and fry well, then mash or grind twice. Pour them back into the frying pan, adding oil, a finely chopped onion, pepper and salt. Fry briefly.

Pour the fried hemp seed over the boiled potatoes, and shake well.

In the Žemaitija region, these potatoes are eaten with sour milk.

Bulvės padaže

*10 potatoes, ½ l milk,
100 g butter, 2 tbsps wheat
flour, 2 onions, 2 tbsps
dill seeds, 2 eggs, salt.*

Potatoes in Sauce

Peel and slice the potatoes, pouring hot milk over them, and adding salt, cooking everything until tender.

Finely chop the onions, and sauté in butter. To the sautéed onions add flour, beaten eggs, and dill seeds. Cook briefly, and add everything to the boiled potatoes.

Serve hot for lunch or in the afternoon with sauerkraut or pickles.

Sauces Served with Potatoes

Onion Sauce

Svogūnų mirkalas

*½ l thick sour cream,
3 onions, pepper, salt.*

Finely chop the onions, and add to the sour cream along with ground pepper and salt. Mix thoroughly, and let stand for 2–3 hrs.

This sauce goes well with potatoes boiled in their skins.

Hemp Seed Sauce

Kanapių padažas

*1 cup hemp seed, 50 g butter,
1 onion, 1 boiled potato,
ground pepper, salt.*

Soak the hemp seed in water for 2–3 hrs. Then pour off the water, grind twice through a meat grinder. Grind the onion, and sauté in butter. Also grind the potato. Put everything into a bowl, adding salt and pepper and mixing thoroughly.

This goes well with hot potatoes boiled in their skins.

Mashed Potato Sauce

Makalas

*4 boiled potatoes, 200 g sour cream,
200 g sour milk, pepper, salt.*

Boil the potatoes and mash while still hot, adding the sour cream and sour milk. Mix everything thoroughly, adding pepper and salt.

This sauce goes well with hot potatoes boiled in their skins. It is also served with mashed potatoes.

Sour Cream Sauce

Grietinės padažas

*½ l sour cream, 1 finely
grated onion, pepper, salt.*

Put everything into a bowl, and mix with a wooden spoon.

This sauce goes well with hot potatoes boiled in their skins.

Mint Sauce

Mėtų mirkalas

*½ l milk, 2 tbsps finely chopped
mint, 2 tbsps melted butter,
1 tbsp flour, 1 onion, pepper, salt.*

Mix the flour in a small amount of cold milk, and pour into boiling milk while constantly stirring. Add the mint, pepper, butter, finely chopped onion, and salt. Bring to a boil.

Serve mint sauce as a separate dish with hot boiled potatoes.

Red Sauce

Raudonas padažas

*½ l beet brine, 1 tbsp flour,
1 onion, pepper, salt.*

Slowly heat the beet brine over a low flame, and while stirring, carefully add the flour, a finely grated onion, ground pepper, and salt. Bring to a boil.

This goes well with potatoes boiled in their skins.

Beet Brine Sauce

Rasalynė

*2 boiled pickled beets,
½ l beet brine, 2 onions, salt.*

Dice the beets. Finely chop the onions, add salt and the diced beets, and pour over with the brine. Mix thoroughly.

This goes well with hot baked potatoes.

Herring Brine

Silkių rasalas

2 herrings, 2 onions, 1 cup beet brine, 3 tbsps cooking oil.

Peel the herring, put into a pan, add a drop of water, and sprinkle with finely chopped onions. Put into a hot oven, and bake for 5–10 min. Remove the bones from the baked herring, cut into small pieces, and mash with a wooden spoon, adding the oil and brine and mixing thoroughly.

This goes well with hot potatoes baked or boiled in their skins.

Linseed Salt

Sėmeninė druska

1 cup linseed, 1 onion, salt.

Toast the linseed in a dry frying pan, and then mash or grind with a meat grinder, adding salt and a finely chopped onion. This goes well with hot baked or boiled potatoes in their skins.

Linseed Salt with Rye Flour

Sėmenų druska su ruginiais miltais

1 cup linseed, 1 onion, 2 tbsps rye flour, salt.

Toast the linseed in a frying pan together with the rye flour until golden brown. Mash the mixture, adding a finely chopped onion and salt.

This goes well with hot potatoes.

Rye Flour Salt

Ruginių miltų druska

1 cup rye flour, 1 onion, 4–5 cloves garlic, salt.

Toast the flour in a dry frying pan with finely chopped garlic and onions. Add salt.

Sprinkle over potatoes.

Hemp Seed Salt

Kanapių druska

1 cup hemp seed, 1 onion, salt.

Fry the hemp seed in a dry frying pan together with a chopped onion, adding salt. Fry until it begins to brown. Then pour into a mortar and grind.

Serve with hot potatoes. Use it in sauerkraut, or use to season other dishes. It is especially good sprinkled over herring or herring dishes.

Salt made from hemp seed is considered tastier than that made from linseed. It is especially valued in the Žemaitija region. It is also called hemp seed tobacco (kanapių tabokas).

Potato Sauce with Sour Milk

Patermesas

2 boiled potatoes, 2 tbsps sour cream, ½ cup sour milk, 1 tsp caraway seeds, 1 onion, salt.

Boil the potatoes, mashing them while still hot, and adding the sour cream and sour milk. Mix everything thoroughly. Then add the caraway seeds, chopped onion, and salt, again mixing well.

In the Žemaitija region, people serve this with hot boiled potatoes in their skins.

Dairy-Free Potato Sauce

"Čiolakas"

4 boiled potatoes, 2 onions, ½ cup potato broth, ground pepper, dill, green onions, salt.

Peel the potatoes and boil in salted water, pouring off the broth, but not throwing it out. Mash the potatoes, adding finely chopped and salted onions, and ground pepper. Pour hot potato broth over it, adding finely chopped dill and green onions. Mix well.

In the Dzūkija region, it is served in summer with hot potatoes in the afternoon or for supper.

Cottage Cheese Sauce

Varškės padažas

200 g cottage cheese, 200 g sour cream or milk, dill sprigs or mint leaves, salt.

Mash the cottage cheese well, mixing it with the sour cream or milk, and adding chopped dill or mint, and salt. Mix well.

This goes well with potatoes or dishes made from potatoes.

Egg Sauce

Kiaušinių padažas

1 tbsp butter, 2 hard-boiled eggs, 1 tbsp lemon balm, 100 g sour cream, salt.

Melt the butter, adding chopped eggs, chopped lemon balm leaves, sour cream, and salt. Heat briefly.

Pour this sauce over hot potatoes.

Hemp Seed Curds

Žildinys

1 cup hemp seed, 1 onion, 2 cups water, salt.

Mash the hemp seed, adding water. When mixed well, a liquid results. Slowly heat this liquid while constantly stirring until it curdles. After removing from the flame, add a finely chopped onion and salt, and mix thoroughly.

This goes well with potatoes or porridges.

Mustard

"Muštarda"

2 tbsps mashed or ground mustard flour, 1 cup water, salt.

Pour boiling water over the mustard flour, and mix well, adding salt. Keep at room temperature for a few days to "add some punch". After standing, this mixture is both bitter and a bit sour.

This sauce is very popular in the Dzūkija region.

Fermented Sauce

Raugalienė

3 cups coarse rye flour, 1 l water.

Mix the rye flour in a pot with water. Put into a hot oven, and cook (with the heat turned off) while the oven cools. A thick mash will form. Dilute with cold boiled water, mix thoroughly, and set out to ferment. It ferments in 2–3 days.

When diluted, the fermented sauce can be used as a beverage when having baked potatoes. When undiluted, it can serve as a sauce.

Fermented sauce can also be used in making soups from beets or sorrel.

Fermented Sauce with Apples

Degtienė
2 cups coarse rye flour, a handful of dried apples, 1 tbsp sugar, 2 cups water.

Pour warm boiled water over the rye flour, adding the apples after rehydrating them and cutting them into strips. Add sugar, mix thoroughly, and put in a warm place to ferment for 2 days.

This goes well with boiled potatoes in their skins.

Beet and Onion Sauce

"Šmotalas"
3 boiled potatoes, 2 onions, 1 clove garlic, 2 tbsps sour cream, 1 cup sour milk, 2 small boiled pickled beets, ground pepper, salt.

Mash the boiled potatoes. Mix the mashed potatoes with the sour cream, adding the sour milk, pepper and salt. Finely chop the onions and garlic, cutting the beets into strips. Mix well.

In the Žemaitija region, beet and onion sauce is served with hot boiled potatoes in their skins in the afternoon or for dinner.

Pickles with Sour Cream

Agurkai su grietine
3 pickles, 200 g sour cream.

Finely dice the pickles, adding the sour cream, and mixing well.

Serve with variously prepared potatoes and potato dishes.

Served with potatoes, this sauce is especially popular in the Aukštaitija region.

White Sauce

Pamirkalas
2 cups milk, 2 tbsps flour, 100 g butter.

Melt the butter in a frying pan, adding the flour to the milk, butter, and mixing well. Heat while constantly stirring until thick.

This can be used for various potato dishes.

Mushroom Sauce

Grybainis
½ l salted mushrooms, 1 onion, 2 cups milk, 2 tbsps cooking oil, 1 boiled potato, ground pepper, 1 tsp chopped oregano, salt.

Soak the salted mushrooms well. Then boil in milk, and grind. Also grind the potato. Finely chop or grind the onion, and sauté in oil.

Put everything into a bowl, and add ground pepper and chopped oregano, mixing well.

Put the mushroom sauce on hot boiled potatoes and serve for lunch.

Sauerkraut Juice with Mushrooms

Kopūstų rūgštis su grybais
1 cup salted mushrooms, 1 onion, ½ cup sauerkraut juice, ground pepper, salt.

Soak the mushrooms well, boil, and cut into little strips. Finely chop the onion, add ground pepper and sauerkraut juice, mixing well.

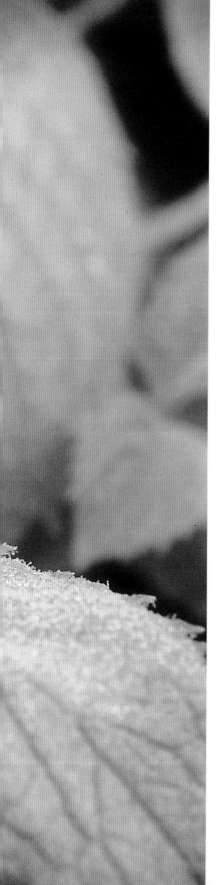

milk

Lithuanian Farmer's Cheese

Lietuviškas varškės sūris

10 l naturally soured milk,
½ cup caraway seeds, salt.

Place a bowl with soured milk into another, larger pot with warm (30–35 °C) water, and warm very carefully over a low flame until the milk rises nicely and becomes frothy (but does not form tiny lumps).

The curds are juicier and tastier when milk is warmed for a longer time at a lower temperature. Pour the warmed milk into a sieve lined with cheese-cloth. After the whey is drained off, add caraway seeds and salt to the curds. Mix thoroughly. Pour the curds into a damp cheesecloth bag, and press for 10–12 hr.

Serve sour milk cheeses fresh, or dry them.

Sour Cream Butter

Kastinys

1 l sour cream, 1 tsp butter,
½ cup caraway seeds, salt.

Put the butter and 1 tablespoon of sour cream into an earthenware bowl that is being warmed in hot water, and stir with a wooden spoon. After stirring a while (before the buttermilk separates), add another spoonful of sour cream, and continue stirring until all the sour cream has been added. Towards the end of the stirring, there should be a homogeneous whitish mixture. When this mixture begins to thicken, add the caraway seeds (after washing and drying), salt heavily, and mix well.

Spoon the sour cream butter into little bowls, and put in a cool place for 2–3 hrs. Sour cream butter has a mildly sour taste because the buttermilk does not separate. This taste is different than sour cream or butter. Sour cream butter is a very popular traditional food in the Žemaitija region, where it is made with various seasonings, for example, by adding mint instead of caraway seeds. They also use allspice, garlic, poppy seeds, and green onions.

Serve sour cream butter with hot boiled potatoes in their skins or black or whole wheat bread, or serve with other dishes.

Sour Cheese

"Kėžas"

1 l soured milk,
100 g sour cream, salt.

Heat the naturally soured milk over a very low flame. After it has risen, pour the heated milk into a sieve or cheesebag so that the liquid drains off. Spoon the curds into a bowl (preferably earthenware), and stir well with a wooden spoon so that a fluffy mass forms. Then add the sour cream, add salt to taste, and continue stirring. Milk can be used instead of sour cream.

This cheese is popular in the Žemaitija region, where it is eaten in the afternoon or for dinner. It is made with various seasonings.

Sour Cheese with Caraway Seeds

"Kėžas" su kmynais

*200 g cottage cheese,
100 g sour cream, ½ cup
caraway seeds, salt.*

Boil the caraway seeds for 5 min., and let dry. Put the cottage cheese into an earthenware bowl, add the sour cream, and mix very well. Towards the end of mixing, add the caraway seeds and salt.

Serve with boiled potatoes in their skins.

Sour Cheese with Poppy Seeds

"Kėžas" su aguonomis

*200 g cottage cheese,
100 g sour cream,
50 g poppy seeds,
2–3 tbsps honey, salt.*

Put the cottage cheese into a bowl, add the sour cream, and mix well.

Pour hot water over the poppy seeds, and let stand for 1–2 hrs. so that they swell up, then mash in a mortar or grind 2–3 times with a meat grinder. Add the ground poppy seeds to the cottage cheese, along with salt and honey. Mix well.

In the Žemaitija region, people eat cheese with poppy seeds with whole wheat bread, cake, or boiled dough squares (skryliai).

Sour Cheese with Mint

"Kėžas" su mėtomis

*200 g cottage cheese, 100 g cream,
2 tbsps chopped or mashed mint, salt.*

Put everything into an earthenware bowl, and mix well with a wooden spoon.

Serve with potatoes, whole wheat bread, or cake.

Sour Cheese with Seasonings

"Kėžas" su prieskoniais

*200 g cottage cheese, 1 tsp tarragon (not
dried), 1 tsp parsley leaves, 1 tsp mint,
1 cup sour cream, 2 cloves garlic, salt.*

To the cottage cheese add chopped tarragon, parsley, and mint leaves, finely chopped garlic, sour cream, and salt. Mix well with a wooden spoon.

Serve with hot potatoes, or with other foods.

Sour Cheese with Mushrooms

"Kėžas" su grybais

*200 g cottage cheese, 100 g sour
cream, 4–5 dried mushrooms,
2 cloves garlic, salt.*

Mash the cottage cheese well with a wooden spoon in an earthenware bowl.

Soak the dried mushrooms for 2–3 hrs., wash well, and boil. After boiling, wash once more, and slice into thin strips. Add finely chopped garlic, mushrooms, and sour cream to the mashed cottage cheese. Add salt, and mix thoroughly.

Serve with hot boiled or baked potatoes.

Sour Cheese with Garlic

"Kėžas" su česnaku

*200 g cottage cheese,
100 g sour cream, 1 tbsp finely
mashed garlic, salt.*

Put the cottage cheese, sour cream, garlic, and salt into a bowl, and mash well.

Serve with hot boiled or baked potatoes in their skins, or spread on black bread.

Baked Cottage Cheese Cakes

Kepti varškėčiai

*400 g cottage cheese,
1 cup flour, 2 eggs, 100 g butter,
100 g sour cream, vanilla sugar,
mint leaves, salt.*

Add the eggs, flour, vanilla sugar, and salt to the cottage cheese, kneading well. From this dough make little rolls the thickness of a finger (2–3 cm), flatten slightly, and slice into pieces 3–4 cm long. Put these pieces into a baking pan, and bake in a hot oven (220 °C) until golden brown.

Melt the butter in a frying pan, add the sour cream, salt, and finely chopped mint leaves, and mix thoroughly. Heat the mixture, but do not bring it to a boil.

After baking, put the cottage cheese cakes into a bowl, pouring the sauce over it.

Seasoned Butter

Sviestas su prieskoniais

*200 g butter, 1 onion, 2 cloves garlic,
1 tbsp grated horseradish, 2–3 dill
sprigs, 2 peppercorns, salt.*

Finely grate the onion, garlic, and horseradish. Finely chop the dill, add to the butter, and add salt. Mix well.

It can be spread on black bread, or served with boiled potatoes in their skins.

Butter with Garlic and Cheese

Sviestas su česnaku ir sūriu

*100 g butter, 3 cloves garlic, 1 small piece
dried farmer's cheese, salt.*

Finely grate the garlic and cheese into the butter, add salt, and mix well.

It can be used as a spread on bread.

Cottage Cheese with Sour Cream

Varškė su grietine

*200 g cottage cheese,
1 cup sweet cream or
sour cream, salt.*

Mash the cottage cheese well with a spoon, add the sour cream and salt, and mix thoroughly.

In the Aukštaitija region, people prepare cottage cheese this way with bread or boiled potatoes, or serve it as a sauce with pancakes.

Česnakinė varškė

200 g cottage cheese,
1 cup sour cream,
3–4 cloves garlic, salt.

Cottage Cheese with Garlic

Finely chop the garlic, mixing salt with it. Add this to the cottage cheese, and mix thoroughly. Then add the sour cream, mixing well.

In the Aukštaitija region, cottage cheese is prepared this way and served in the afternoon or for dinner. They serve it with hot boiled or baked potatoes.

Varškė su peletrūnu

200 g cottage cheese,
1 cup milk,1 tbsp tarragon, salt.

Cottage Cheese with Tarragon

Mash the cottage cheese, adding the milk, finely chopped tarragon, and salt. Mix well.

Eat with hot boiled or baked potatoes, potato pancakes, or serve with kugel.

Varškė su duona

100 g cottage cheese,
½ cup cream, 1 cup dried black
bread cubes, 1 tbsp boiled caraway
seeds, mint leaves, salt.

Cottage Cheese with Bread

Mix the cottage cheese well with the cream, adding the caraway seeds and mint leaves. Mix thoroughly. Pour the bread cubes into a bowl, and pour over with the cottage cheese.

Serve with tea or coffee.

Virti varškėčiai

400 g cottage cheese,
2 eggs, 1 cup flour,
100 g butter, 100 g sour
cream, 3 tbsps caraway
seeds, 1 tsp tarragon, salt,
cooking fat or water.

Boiled Cottage Cheese Dumplings

Mash the cottage cheese, adding the eggs, flour, caraway seeds, and salt. Knead thoroughly. From the dough make little rolls the thickness of a finger (2–3 cm), and slice into pieces 1–2 cm long. Put these pieces into heated fat or salted boiling water. Deep-fry in fat until golden brown, or boil in water for 5–10 min.

For cottage cheese dumplings boiled in water, make a butter sauce: melt the butter in a frying pan, adding the sour cream, salt, and finely chopped tarragon. Mix thoroughly.

Remove the cottage cheese dumplings from the water, put into a bowl, and pour over with the sauce. Serve hot.

Remove the cottage cheese dumplings fried in fat, put on a plate, and sprinkle with powdered sugar. They can be eaten hot or after they have cooled off.

Cottage Cheese Dumplings

Varškės kukuliai

400 g cottage cheese, 4 egg whites, 5 tbsps flour, mint or tarragon leaves, salt, cooking fat.

Mash the cottage cheese well, adding stiffly beaten egg whites, chopped mint or tarragon, and salt, mixing thoroughly.

From this mixture make walnut-sized dumplings, roll in flour, and put into boiling fat. Deep-fry until they rise to the surface and puff up. Remove with a slotted spoon.

Eat either warm or cold. Serve with tea, coffee, juice, or kvass.

Cottage cheese dumplings can be made in many different ways. Each time they put something new into the mixture, such as poppy seeds, raisins, dried fruit, berries, mushrooms, or other ingredients.

Colostrum

Krekenos

1 l colostrum (milk from a cow that has recently calved), 100 g butter, 1 cup milk, 1 tbsp chopped oregano, salt.

Add the milk, melted butter, oregano, and salt to the colostrum, mixing well.

Pour this colostrum into an earthenware pot or baking pan, and bake in a moderate oven until golden brown and firm to the touch (for about 15–20 min.).

Serve hot with white or black bread for breakfast.

This is the typical recipe for the Aukštaitija region. In the Dzūkija region, they add a couple of eggs.

In Lithuania, the custom of taking a cow's very first milk to the neighbors to be tasted has remained in some areas.

Colostrum Pancakes

Krekenų blynai

½ l colostrum, 2 cups flour, tarragon or marjoram, salt, cooking fat.

Combine the colostrum and flour, and beat well, adding salt and chopped seasonings. Mix thoroughly. Spoon this mixture into heated fat, and fry on both sides in a frying pan.

Serve with bread for breakfast.

Cheese with Cream

Sūris su grietinėle

200 g dried cheese with caraway seeds, 100 g bread, ½ l cream, 1 tbsp sugar, mint leaves.

Slice the cheese and bread into small cubes. Pour the sugar into a bowl, add the cubed cheese and bread, pour over with cream, and mix thoroughly so that the sugar dissolves. Add chopped mint leaves.

Serve in the afternoon or for dinner.

This dish can also be prepared dish quickly for unexpected guests.

Cheese Rolled in Egg

Sūris, apkeptas su kiaušiniu

*200 g farmer's cheese,
1 egg, 100 g butter,
1 tbsp chopped mint, salt.*

Cut the cheese into thin (1 cm thick) slices. Roll the slices in a well-beaten, salted egg, and fry in hot butter. Put the fried cheese slices into a bowl, and sprinkle with chopped mint.

In the Aukštaitija region, people eat cheese rolled in egg for breakfast.

Baked Farmer's Cheese

Pakepintas varškės sūris

*500 g farmer's cheese, 100 g butter,
1 tbsp mint or tarragon.*

Cut the fresh salted cheese into slices 1–2 cm thick, and put into a baking pan. Sprinkle with crushed mint or tarragon, putting dollops of butter on top. Bake in a slow to moderate oven for 10 min.

In the Aukštaitija region, people eat baked cheese for breakfast.

Baked Cheese with Mint

Pakepintas sūris su mėtomis

*1 cake farmer's cheese,
50 g butter, 2 tbsps finely
chopped mint leaves.*

Poke holes in the fresh cheese with a fork, cover with butter, sprinkle with mint, and bake in an oven until golden brown.

Serve hot with tea or coffee.

Cheese Wrapped in Pastry

Sūris tešloje

*1 cake farmer's cheese,
200 g butter, 100 g sour cream,
2 egg yolks, 3 tbsps sugar,
1 cup raisins, 2 tbsps honey,
20 g vanilla sugar, flour.*

Knead a moderately stiff dough from the butter, sour cream, eggs, flour, and vanilla sugar. Roll out, and sprinkle with raisins that have been washed. On the top of this, put the cake of cheese after poking holes with a fork in the cheese and covering it with honey. Wrap the cheese in the rolled dough, squeezing the edges tightly together.

Put the wrapped cheese into a hot oven (220 °C), and bake until the dough is done (for 25–35 min.).

The cheese baked in a flaky crust can be served either hot or after it has cooled off. Cut into thin slices with a sharp knife, and serve with mint tea.

Baked Dried Cheese

Keptas džiovintas sūris

*1 cake dried farmer's cheese,
100 g butter, ½ tsp black pepper
and allspice, 1 tsp caraway
seeds, 1 tsp tarragon.*

Spread melted butter over the cheese, sprinkling with ground pepper, chopped tarragon, and caraway seeds. Put the cheese into a baking pan, and bake in a moderate oven (180 °C) until soft and golden brown.

After removing, cut the cheese into thin slices.

In the Aukštaitija region, this cheese is served to guests with beer.

Buttermilk with Onions

Pasukienė

*1 l fresh buttermilk,
2 onions, 1 tbsp
tarragon, salt.*

Chop the onions very finely, and put into a bowl, adding salt. Add the tarragon and buttermilk, mix thoroughly.

Serve with porridge (especially grucė, which is made from whole groats) or with boiled, baked, or mashed potatoes.

Baked Cottage Cheese

Kepta varškė

*300 g cottage cheese,
100 g butter, 2 tbsps caraway
seeds, 1 tbsp tarragon,
2 eggs, salt.*

Mash the cottage cheese, adding the butter, eggs, caraway seeds, tarragon, and salt. Mix well, and put into a baking pan greased with butter. Bake in a moderate oven (180 °C) until the cottage cheese is golden brown.

Serve hot poured over with melted butter or honey. Mint, thyme, oregano, or caraway seed tea goes very well with baked cottage cheese.

Cottage Cheese Patties with Potato

Bulviniai varškėčiai

*300 g cottage cheese,
4–5 boiled potatoes, 1 egg,
1 cup flour, 100 g sour cream,
1 tsp crushed thyme,
salt, butter.*

In a bowl, mash the cottage cheese well, adding boiled potatoes mashed, the egg, half a cup of flour, thyme, and salt. Knead everything thoroughly. From this mixture make patties, roll in flour, and fry in heated butter on both sides until golden brown.

Serve with sour cream for breakfast.

Cottage Cheese Dumplings with Bread

Duoniniai varškės kukuliai

*3 cups rye flour, 1 cup buttermilk
or soured milk, 300 g cottage
cheese, 2 eggs, 2 tbsps caraway
seeds, 100 g butter, salt.*

Mash the cottage cheese well in a bowl, adding the eggs, flour, buttermilk or soured milk, caraway seeds, and salt. Knead well, and put in a warm place to rise (for 3–4 hrs.). From the leavened dough make dumplings, and put into salted boiling water. Cook for 5–10 min. Remove from the water, pour over with melted butter.

Serve hot for dinner with herbal tea. The dumplings can also be topped with berry preserves, apple sauce, or honey.

Cottage Cheese Squares with Buckwheat

Grikinis
varškės apkepas

*500 g cottage cheese,
1 cup buckwheat groats,
3 eggs, 200 g butter,
1 cup milk, 200 g sour
cream, 1 tsp tarragon,
salt, 2 cups water.*

Wash the buckwheat groats, and pour into boiling water. Cook for 10 min. Then add the milk and salt, bring to a boil, cover the pot, and put into a hot oven to finish cooking.

Mash the cottage cheese well, add the eggs, and mix thoroughly. Let the boiled groats cool off, add to the cottage cheese, add tarragon, and mix well. Grease a baking pan with butter, spoon in the cottage cheese mixture, making a layer 3–4 cm thick. Put dollops of butter on top, and bake in an oven for 30–40 min. until the top is nicely toasted. While still hot, slice into small squares, put into a bowl, and pour over with a sauce of melted butter and sour cream.

These cottage cheese squares can be made with various ingredients, including oat, rye, wheat, and hulled or pearl barley groats.

This food is popular for breakfast.

Cottage Cheese Casserole with Carrot

Morkinis
varškės apkepas

*500 g cottage cheese,
3 carrots, 3 eggs,
½ cup farina, 3 apples,
3 tbsps sugar, 2 tbsps caraway
seeds, ¼ tsp ground coriander.*

In a bowl mash the cottage cheese well, adding eggs mixed with sugar, butter, finely grated carrots, caraway seeds, and ground coriander. Mix thoroughly. Then add the farina, peeled and finely sliced apples, and salt. Mix well.

Spoon this mixture into a greased baking pan. Bake in a moderate oven (180 °C) for 25–30 min.

Serve this casserole in the same pan in which it was baked. Serve hot with sweet milk, various herbal teas, or fruit juice.

Hedgehogs

Varškės ežiukai

*300 g cottage cheese,
2 eggs, 1 cup flour,
1 tbsp chopped mint,
100 g sour cream,
50 g butter,
salt.*

Mash the cottage cheese in a bowl, adding flour, eggs, chopped mint, and salt, kneading well. From this mixture make finger-thick rolls with a rolling pin, slice into pieces 2–3 cm long. With fingertips press these pieces against the inner side of a fine grater until a hollow roll is formed with the pattern of a hedgehog. If pressed more firmly, the hedgehogs are thinner, cook quicker, and are more delicious.

Put the hedgehogs into boiling salted water, and cook for about 10 min. When done, remove, drain, put into a bowl, and pour over with melted butter and sour cream.

Serve hot.

mushrooms

Fried Mushrooms with Onions

Kepti grybai su svogūnais

½ kg mushroom caps (king boletes, saffron milkcaps, or orange aspen boletes), 200 g cooking oil, 3 onions, pepper, bay leaves, salt.

Wash the mushroom caps well, drain, and put into hot cooking oil, frying over a low flame for about 20 min. Add sliced onions, seasonings, and salt, and let stew a little longer (for about 5 min.).

Fried mushrooms can be eaten either cold or warm. Hot potatoes go well with warm mushrooms, and toasted bread with cold ones.

Fried Saffron Milkcaps with Onions

Pakepintos rudmėsės su svogūnais

½ l saffron milkcaps, 2 tbsps flour, 100 g fat (butter or cooking oil), 4 onions, pepper, salt.

Clean off the saffron milkcaps, put into boiling salted water, and cook for 10 min. Remove from the water, drain, add pepper, roll in flour, and fry in a frying pan with fat.

After frying, put the saffron milkcaps into a bowl, pouring sautéed sliced onions over them.

Serve with boiled potatoes for lunch.

Mushroom Caps Fried in Butter

Grybų kepurėlės, keptos svieste

½ l mushroom caps (king boletes, saffron milkcaps, or orange aspen boletes), 100 g butter, 2 tbsps flour, dill, pepper, salt.

Wash the mushrooms well, drain, and roll in flour mixed with salt and pepper. Fry in butter in a frying pan over a low flame until golden brown (for about 20 min.).

Before serving, sprinkle with chopped dill leaves.

Serve for lunch or in the afternoon with hot potatoes or bread.

Mushroom and Potato Stew

Grybų ir bulvių šutinys

10 potatoes, 1 l mushrooms, 100 g butter, 2 onions, 200 g sour cream, dill or parsley, pepper, salt.

Peel the potatoes, slice into large rectangular pieces, put into boiling water, and cook. When done, drain the potatoes (pour the liquid into a separate container).

Finely chop the onions, and sauté in butter. Clean and wash the mushrooms, boil in salted water for 20 min., and remove from the water. Drain and slice the mushrooms, adding them to the sautéed onions. Stew for 2–3 min., adding pepper and a little of the potato broth. Stew a further 5 min.

Pour the stewed mushrooms over the potatoes, mixing thoroughly. Serve with sour cream poured on top and sprinkled with chopped dill or parsley. Serve for lunch.

Stewed Mushrooms with Sour Cream

Troškinti grybai su grietine

½ l fresh mild mushrooms, 100 g butter, 2 onions, 200 g sour cream, dill, green onions, salt.

Clean off the fresh mushrooms, wash well, slice, and put into a frying pan. Add salt, and stew (covered) in their own juices until these juices evaporate. Then add butter, chopped onion bulbs, and the dill, frying for 15 min. When done, add the sour cream, sprinkle with finely chopped green onions, and stew for 5 min. more.

Serve with bread or hot potatoes for lunch or in the afternoon.

Batter-Fried Mushrooms

Kepti grybai tešloje

½ l mushrooms, 10 g fat, 1 egg, 2 tbsps flour, 2 tbsps bread crumbs, salt.

Wash and drain the mushrooms, slice, add salt, roll in egg batter and bread crumbs. Put into heated fat, and fry on both sides.

After frying, put the mushrooms into a pan, and bake for 10–15 min. in a slow to moderate oven (180 °C).

Serve with bread or hot potatoes for lunch or in the afternoon. In the Dzūkija region, batter-fried mushrooms are also eaten for breakfast.

Mushrooms in Sauce

Grybai padaže

1 cup boiled mushrooms, 2 eggs, 1 cup sour cream, 1 tbsp flour, 1 tbsp caraway seeds, dill, pepper, salt.

Slice the mushrooms into strips. Beat the eggs with the flour, adding the pepper, caraway seeds, and salt. While stirring, add the beaten eggs and mushrooms to the heated sour cream. Heat until the entire mixture thickens.

Sprinkle with chopped dill before serving.

Serve with hot potatoes for lunch.

Fried Dried Mushrooms

Kepti džiovinti grybai

100 g dried mushrooms, 3 tbsps flour, 150 g butter or cooking oil, 1 cup milk, green onions, dill sprigs, salt.

Wash the dried mushrooms well in cold water, and then soak in milk for 3 hr. Wash well with cold water once more, drain, stretching by hand to remove the wrinkles. Add salt, roll in flour, and fry in heated butter or cooking oil on all sides for about 15–20 min.

When the mushrooms are done, put on a plate, pour over with the butter or cooking oil in which they were fried, and sprinkle with chopped green onions and dill sprigs.

Serve hot with bread.

Mushroom Sauce

Grybų padažas

5 dried mushrooms, 50 g butter, 1 tbsp flour, 1 cup mushroom broth, ½ cup sour cream, salt.

Soak the dried mushrooms in water for 2–3 hrs. Boil in the same liquid they were soaked in. When done, slice the mushrooms into strips. Fry the flour in butter, dilute with the mushroom broth, and heat while stirring until thick. Then add the sliced mushrooms, sour cream, and salt, and continue heating a little longer.

Serve with hot potatoes or mashed potatoes

Mushroomers' Roast

Grybautojų kepsnys

10 king boletes or orange aspen, boletes, 3 onions, garlic, salt.

Wipe the mushrooms clean, sprinkle on all sides with salt and pepper, and thread on a metal skewer or sharp stick. Alternate a mushroom and a thick slice of onion until the ingredients are used up. Roast over the embers of a fire for about 20 min.

Salted Mushroom Patties

Sūdytų grybų maltiniai

1 l salted mushrooms, 3 eggs, 2 tbsps sour cream, 2 onions, 200 g butter, 1 tbsp flour, 1 cup bread crumbs, ground pepper, 2 cloves garlic, salt.

Soak the mushrooms well, changing the water several times. Wash, drain, and finely chop or grind. To the mushrooms add the eggs, sour cream, chopped onions sautéed in 2 tbsps of butter, bread crumbs, finely chopped garlic, ground pepper, and salt. Mix well, and let stand for 30 min. for the bread crumbs to swell up.

From this mixture make patties, roll in flour, and fry in heated butter for 25–30 min. Serve hot for lunch with hot potatoes and pickles.

Ears with Mushroom Filling

Ausytės su grybų įdaru

3 cups flour, 3 eggs, 2 cups fresh or dried ground mushrooms, 1 onion, 2 tbsps butter, 2 tbsps sour cream, water, pepper, salt.

Pour the flour into a bowl, add 2 eggs, a little water, and a pinch of salt. Knead the dough as for pasta (rather stiff). Roll the dough thin, and cut into little squares. On each of them put some mushroom filling, fold over into a triangle, squeeze the edges together with a fork or your fingers, and join the 2 corners together.

For the filling, add an egg, a finely chopped onion sautéed in butter, pepper, and salt to the ground mushrooms, mixing well.

Boil in salted water for 5–7 min. Remove the ears, drain, put into a bowl, and pour butter boiled with sour cream and salt over them. Another option is to sprinkle with hemp seed and linseed salt, or pour hemp seed and poppy seed milk over them.

Mushroom Cake

Grybų tortas

*1 l mushrooms, 3 raw eggs,
2 hard-boiled eggs,
4 tbsps bread crumbs,
1 cup sour cream, 2 onions,
2 tbsps flour, pepper,
50 g cooking oil, salt.*

Clean and wash the mushrooms, and partially boil. Remove, drain, and slice, adding finely chopped onions sautéed in cooking oil, chopped hard-boiled eggs, bread crumbs, pepper, salt, and the raw eggs. Mix well.

Grease a cake form, filling it with the mixture. Sprinkle flour on top, and bake in a moderate oven (180 °C) for 30 min.

Pour sour cream over the hot mushroom cake, and serve with hot potatoes.

Mushroom cake can also be served after it has cooled off as a snack with fried black or white bread.

In the Žemaitija region, this cake is served with sour cream butter.

King Bolete Cheese

Baravykų sūris

*1 l fresh king boletes,
3 onions, 4 hard-boiled eggs,
3 raw eggs, 2 tbsps caraway
seeds, 2–3 peppercorns,
100 g butter, salt.*

Clean, wash, and slice the king boletes, partially cooking in salted water. Remove from the water, drain, and grind. Chop the hard-boiled eggs. Finely chop the onions, and sauté in butter. Put everything into a bowl, adding the raw eggs, salt, caraway seeds, and ground pepper, mixing thoroughly.

Put this mixture into a double cheesecloth bag, and boil in water for 5–10 min. Then remove from the water, and press.

King bolete cheese is a holiday treat and adorns the table during celebrations. It is garnished with various fresh vegetables.

Mushrooms in Eggs

Grybai kiaušiniuose

*8 eggs, 5 mushroom caps,
1 cup boiled ground mushrooms,
1 cup sour cream, 100 g butter,
ground pepper, green
onions, dill, salt.*

Hard-boil 7 of the eggs. Cut the tops off 5 of them, and remove the yolks.

Sprinkle the mushroom caps with salt, and fry in butter.

Finely chop the other 2 hard-boiled eggs and the 5 removed yolks, adding them to the boiled ground mushrooms along with the one raw egg. Mix everything thoroughly, and stew in butter with the seasonings and salt for 10 min.

Put this mixture into the eggs from which the yolks were removed, cut off their bottoms so that they can stand on end, and put the mushroom caps on top.

Pour sour cream mixed with salt into a shallow bowl, sprinkle with finely chopped green onions and dill, and neatly stand the eggs on end.

Serve as a snack with fried black or white bread.

Fresh Mushrooms with Herring

Švieži grybai su silke

½ l mushrooms, 1 herring, 1 pickle, 2 onions, 200 g sour cream or 4–5 tbsps salad oil, dill, pepper, salt.

Clean and wash the mild fresh mushrooms, and boil for 15–20 min. in salted water with the seasonings (1 chopped onion, dill sprigs with the stem, pepper). When done, pour the mushrooms into a colander to drain off the water, and when cool, slice into narrow strips. After soaking, peel the herring, remove the bones, and slice into small pieces. Mix the mushrooms with the herring, a finely chopped onion, and a finely sliced pickle. Put the mushrooms into a salad bowl, and pour salad oil or sour cream over it.

Garnish the salad with mushroom caps, hard-boiled eggs, and green vegetables.

Serve as a snack with bread or with boiled or baked potatoes.

Mushroom Omelette

Grybų omletas

1 cup fresh, pickled, or salted mushrooms, 3 eggs, 3 tbsps milk, 50 g butter, 1 tbsp flour, 1 onion, pepper, salt, parsley leaves.

If the mushrooms are fresh, clean off well, wash, and cook. If salted or pickled mushrooms are being used, soak very well in cold water, and wash off. Slice the mushrooms into narrow strips. Finely chop the onion, put into melted butter along with the sliced mushrooms, and sauté.

Beat the eggs well, add pepper, salt, flour, and milk. Beat well, and pour this mixture over the mushrooms. Fry on both sides over a low flame.

When done, put the mushroom omelette on a plate, and sprinkle with parsley leaves and hemp seed or linseed salt.

Baked Mushrooms with Bread

Grybų apkepas su duona

½ l fresh or salted mushrooms, ½ l bread crumbs, 1 onion, 100 g butter, 2 eggs, 2 tbsps flour, pepper, 1 tbsp caraway seeds, 2–3 cloves garlic, salt.

Clean, wash, and partially cook the fresh mushrooms. If salted mushrooms are being used, soak and wash well. Grind the mushrooms, or chop very finely.

Finely chop the onion, put into melted butter, and sauté until golden brown, then add bread crumbs, and continue sautéing while stirring.

Add bread crumbs, caraway seeds, ground pepper, finely chopped garlic, and salt to the ground mushrooms, mixing well.

Beat the eggs well with the flour.

Spoon this mixture into a baking pan greased with butter, pour the beaten eggs on top.

Bake in a moderate oven for 20–25 min.

Serve a salad of fresh or pickled vegetables with baked mushrooms.

Grybų ir grikių apkepas

½ l fresh mild mushrooms,
1 cup buckwheat groats,
200 g butter, 100 g sour cream,
1 onion, salt, ½ cup water.

Baked Mushrooms with Buckwheat

Clean the mushrooms, wash well, put into a frying pan in which a finely chopped onion was sautéed in 100 g of butter, cover, and stew for 10–15 min. When almost done, add the sour cream.

To boiling salted water add 50 g of butter and the buckwheat groats, boil until a loose porridge is made. Grease a baking pan with butter (50 g), spoon in the buckwheat porridge after mixing with the mushrooms, and bake for 10–15 min. in an oven.

Grybų makalynė

½ l marinated or salted mushrooms,
2 onions, 2 boiled potatoes,
2–3 cloves garlic, pepper,
1 boiled carrot, 1 pickle, salt,
½ cup cooking oil.

Mushroom Salad

Wash the mushrooms well, soak well if needed, and slice into strips. Dice the potatoes, carrot, and pickle. Cut the onion into thin slices, and sauté in cooking oil. Finely chop the garlic.

Put all these ingredients into a bowl, add salt, and mix well. Serve as a snack with bread.

This mixture goes well with herring, fish dishes, or stewed potatoes.

Voveraičių troškinys

1 l chanterelles, 200 g butter,
5 potatoes, 2 onions, 2 carrots,
2 cloves garlic, 1 dill stem with the
sprigs, 1 cup sour cream, salt.

Chanterelle Stew

Wash the chanterelles well, and chop finely. Finely chop the onions, sauté in butter, pour into a bowl, add the chanterelles, diced potatoes, coarsely grated carrots, chopped garlic, and the entire stem of dill with the seeds (remove the smaller sprigs). Add salt. Stew everything until the potatoes are tender (for 20–25 min.). When almost done, add the sour cream, and bring to a boil.

Sprinkle the stew with finely chopped dill sprigs.

Serve for lunch with bread and cucumbers or pickles.

Keptos voveraitės

1 l chanterelles, 100 g butter,
2 onions, ground pepper,
dill, salt, green onions.

Fried Chanterelles

Wash the chanterelles, put into boiling salted water, and cook for 15 min. Remove from the water, and drain.

Finely chop the onions, sauté in butter, adding the chanterelles, ground pepper, and salt. Fry for 10 min. in a covered frying pan, stirring occasionally. When almost done, add chopped dill and green onions.

Serve for lunch with hot potatoes.

fish

Dried Smelt and Other Small Fish

Džiovintos stintos
ir kitos smulkios
žuvytės

Gut the fish, and wipe out with a rag. Then in a bowl, add salt and seasonings (juniper berries, coriander seeds, oregano, pepper, bay leaves), using a lot of salt. Let stand for 48 hrs. Then pour off the brine, dry the fish, run a string or wire through their eyes, and dry in a sunny covered place with good air circulation or in a slow to moderate oven (180 °C). Well-dried fish can be kept in a dry room for a very long time.

Dried fish are very good when cooked with unsalted potato soup or when just snacked on. Serve cold. Fish soup can be made with barley groats, potatoes, cabbage, and beets, or stew with potatoes or other vegetables.

Salted Vimba

Sūdyti žiobriai

Do not scale the vimba, only gut, and wash well. Then put into a wooden or enamel bowl, adding plenty of salt (mix the salt with ground pepper, coriander seeds, crushed bay, sage, and oregano leaves, juniper berries, cardamon seeds). The next day pour off the brine, firmly press down the vimba in the bowl, and keep in a cold room.

When preparing a meal, soak the salted vimba in cold water, and make fish soup, or stew in fat with carrots and dill.

Serve with boiled potatoes in their skins.

Salted Bleak with Yellow Knight Mushrooms

Sūdytos aukšlės
su žaliuokėmis

Gut the bleak, salt heavily in an enamel bowl, press down. Keep this way for 48 hrs.

Clean off the yellow knights, and partially cook for 10–15 min. After pouring off the water, add salt.

After two days pour off the fish brine, layer the fish with seasonings (dill stems with the seeds, juniper berries, sage, peppercorns, and bay leaves) and mushrooms in a wooden keg, earthenware crock, or enamel container. When the container is full, press down, and on top add a layer of oil 3–5 cm deep. Cover the container with a lid, and keep in a cold room.

Bleak and yellow knights prepared in this way, with sliced onions added, can be served with boiled potatoes or black bread. Sometimes sour cream is also added.

This particular way of salting fish is popular in eastern Lithuania.

Kepti karosai

1 kg crucian carp, 2–3 cloves garlic, crushed southernwood leaves, salt, cooking oil.

Fried Crucian Carp

Clean and wash the crucian carp, and remove the gills, but do not cut into pieces. Rub the insides with crushed garlic, chopped southernwood, and salt. Let stand for 1 hr. in a cool place. Fry in heated fat until both sides are golden brown.

Serve with baked or boiled potatoes and pickles.

Keptas ungurys

1 kg eel, 1 lemon, seasonings (pepper, bay leaves, marjoram, cloves), parsley leaves, salt.

Baked Eel

Peel, clean, and dry the eel. Rub with ground seasonings and salt. Fry young eels without peeling, cleaning the skin well, and rubbing with salt.

After preparing, put the eel into a baking pan unsliced, and bake in a moderate oven for 30 min. while basting with the juices that form from it.

When done, slice the eel into small pieces, put onto a plate, and garnish with slices of lemon and parsley leaves.

Serve as a snack with black bread or toasted white bread.

Grybais įdarytas keptas upėtakis

1 kg trout, 20 g dried king boletes, 2 onions, 200 g butter, 3 tbsps sour cream, marjoram, herbs (carrot, celery, parsley root, leek, lovage), 3 tbsps flour, dill sprigs, salt.

Baked Trout Stuffed with Mushrooms

Slit the trout open below the neck, clean out, wash, dry, and rub the insides with salt and marjoram.

To make the filling, soak the king boletes in cold water for 2–3 hrs. Then boil in the same water, remove, slice, adding finely chopped onions sautéed in butter, sour cream, and salt. Mix well. Stuff the trout with this mixture, and sew up the slits. Roll the trout in flour, and partially fry in heated butter. Set the trout in a greased baking pan with their backs upward, sprinkle with chopped herbs, putting dollops of butter on the trout, and adding very little water. Bake for 10–15 min. in a moderate oven (180 °C), then add the mushroom broth, and continue baking for another 10–15 min., while constantly basting with the liquid in which the trout are being baked.

When done, carefully remove the trout, pull out the threads, put onto a plate, adding the herbs and liquid from the baking pan. Sprinkle with chopped dill.

Serve the trout hot with boiled potatoes or green salads.

This dish is often served during the holidays.

Baked Pike in White Sauce

Kepta lydeka baltame padaže

1 kg pike, 100 g butter, 1 tbsp flour, ½ cup sour cream, 1 lemon, thyme, pepper, salt.

Clean the pike, but do not slice, only wipe dry, and rub with pepper, crushed thyme, and salt. Put the fish into a frying pan with heated butter, pour over with flour beaten in a mixture of sour cream and lemon juice, and bake in a moderate oven for 25–30 min., basting with the same sauce.

When done, carefully put the pike, unsliced, on a platter, or carefully cut into pieces, pouring the same sauce in which it was baked over the pike.

Serve hot with boiled or mashed potatoes.

Fried Fish in Rye Dough

Kepta žuvis ruginių miltų tešloje

1 kg fish, 2 cups rye flour, 1 pickle, 1 egg, thyme, cooking fat, ½ cup water, pepper, salt.

Clean and wash the fish, slice into pieces, and sprinkle with salt, ground pepper, and crushed thyme.

Knead some dough from the rye flour, egg, and water, and wrap the pieces of fish in it. Fry in a large amount of oil until all sides are golden brown.

Fry pike or any other lean fish in this way.

When done, put the fish on a plate, garnish with sliced pickles.

Serve with baked or boiled potatoes. Stewed sauerkraut or pickled beets are sometimes served with it.

Fried Fish with Horseradish Sauce

Kepta žuvis su krienų padažu

1 kg pike, tench, cod, or other large fish, 1 egg, 50 g bread crumbs, oregano, pepper, salt, 2 tbsps sugar, cooking oil, 100 g horseradish, 1 pickle, 1 cup sour cream.

Clean and wash the fish, dry off well, slice into pieces, and add salt. Rub with ground pepper and oregano, soak in a beaten egg, and roll in the crumbs. Fry in a frying pan in a large amount of heated oil, turning over repeatedly until golden brown.

When done, put on a plate, and garnish with sliced pickles.

Finely grate the horseradishes, adding salt, sugar, and sour cream, and mixing thoroughly. Serve the horseradish in a separate bowl.

Serve with baked or boiled potatoes for lunch.

Fried Tench

Keptas lynas

1 kg tench, 2 tbsps flour, 2 tsps oregano, 20 g green onions, salt, cooking oil.

Clean, wash, and dry the tench, cut into small pieces, adding salt, and rubbing with oregano. Roll the fish in flour, and fry in oil until golden brown.

Put on a plate, and sprinkle with finely sliced green onions.

Serve with sauerkraut, horseradish, or green vegetable salads.

Meškeriotojų žuvis

1 fresh fish, 50 g butter,
1 onion, peppercorns,
2–3 juniper berries, salt.

Anglers' Fish

Clean the fish, remove the gills, and wash well. Crush the juniper berries and peppercorns, mix with salt, and rub onto the insides of the fish. Slice the onion, and put inside the fish with small dollops of butter. On the outside of the fish, rub in a little more salt.

After preparation, wrap the fish in clean paper or foil, place among the embers of a fire, and bake for 25–30 min. After removing from the embers, let cool, and unwrap.

Serve with black bread or with hot potatoes baked in the same embers.

Meškeriotojų kepsnys

1 kg small fish or sliced large fish,
4–5 onions, juniper berries,
peppercorns, thyme, salt.

Anglers' Roast

Clean and wash the small fish well, but do not slice, and do not cut off the heads. Rub the insides of the fish with crushed pepper, juniper berries, and thyme mixed with salt.

Pierce the fish through the eyes with a metal or wooden spit. In the spaces between the fish, skewer slices of onion 1 cm thick. Roast over a fire with a low flame.

If you are roasting a larger fish, cut without scaling into slices 1–1,5 cm thick, and rub with crushed pepper, thyme, and juniper berries mixed with salt on both sides. Skewer a slice of fish on a metal or wooden spit, next to it press a slice of onion, and then another slice and so on until the ingredients have been used up. Roast over a fire.

Serve with black garlic bread or with potatoes baked in the same fire.

Daržovėmis įdaryta kepta lydeka

1 kg pike, 1 onion,
1 small celery root, 1 carrot,
1 parsley root, 1 hard-boiled egg,
200 g butter, 1 uncooked egg,
parsley leaves, pepper, salt.

Baked Pike Stuffed with Vegetables

Clean the fish, remove the gills, and wash.

Finely chop the onions, and sauté in butter. Coarsely grate a parsley root and add it, along with celery, and a carrot. Sauté for 2–3 min. Add a chopped hard-boiled egg and a raw egg, along with salt and ground pepper. Mix thoroughly.

Spoon the filling into the pike, and sew up. Melt the butter in a baking pan, and place the stuffed pike in the pan. Bake in a moderate oven (180 °C) for 30–45 min., occasionally basting with the butter.

When done, put the pike, unsliced, on a platter, and sprinkle with parsley leaves.

Serve cold with horseradish sauce.

Fish Stewed in Beet Brine

Burokėlių rasale šutinta žuvis

*1 kg pike or other large fish,
½ l beet brine, 2 onions,
1 carrot, 1 uncooked beet,
½ cup sour cream,
1 tbsp flour, 20 g butter,
1 tsp caraway seeds,
1 parsley root, 1 bay leaf, 1 sprig
of oregano, pepper, green
onions or dill, salt.*

Add a sliced carrot, sliced onions, a coarsely grated beet, parsley, seasonings, and salt to the beet brine, and cook until tender. Strain the broth.

Clean, scale, and dry off the pike. Rub with caraway seeds and salt, and put into a pot. Pour over with the broth, and stew over a low flame for 25–30 min. When almost done, add flour sautéed in butter, and sour cream.

Put the cooked fish into a bowl, cut into pieces, pour over with the sauce in which it was cooked, and sprinkle with chopped greens. Garnish with boiled potatoes.

Any fresh large fish can be stewed in this way.

Serve with hot boiled potatoes for lunch.

Carp Stewed in Cream

Grietinėlėje troškintas karpis

*1 kg carp, 1 egg, 200 g cream,
200 g butter, pepper, bay leaves,
thyme, tarragon, vegetables (1 onion,
carrot, parsley root, celery stalk,
and leek), bread crumbs, salt.*

Clean, wash, and dry the carp. Cut into pieces, rub with salt, dip into a beaten egg, roll in the crumbs, and partially fry in butter. Then put into a pot with melted butter, add the cream, chopped herbs, and vegetables, and stew over a low flame for 25–30 min.

Serve hot, drizzled with the bouillon in which it was cooked and sprinkled with parsley leaves.

Serve with boiled or mashed potatoes.

Boiled Tench or Bream

Virti lynai arba karšiai

*1 kg tench or bream, ½ lemon,
marjoram, pepper, salt, vegetables
(1 onion, carrot, parsley root,
small celery stalk).
FOR THE SAUCE:
2 tbsps butter, ½ cup grated
horseradish, 1 tbsp flour,
½ cup bouillon, ½ cup sour
cream, ½ lemon, sugar, salt.*

Clean and wash the fish, rub the insides with salt, and drizzle with lemon juice. Then cut the fish into pieces, and put into a pot, adding the seasonings and sliced vegetables, and enough water to barely cover the fish. Without covering the pot, slowly bring to a boil, and cook for 20 min.

To make the sauce, briefly sauté the flour in butter, adding the horseradish, and diluting with vegetable bouillon. Squeeze in the lemon juice, add salt, and bring to a boil over a low flame. Add the sour cream, and mix thoroughly.

When done, carefully remove the fish, put on a plate, pouring the liquid in which it was boiled over onto the fish.

Serve for lunch with boiled potatoes and hot horseradish sauce.

Virtas karšis su krienais

1 kg bream, ½ cup grated horseradish, 2 autumn or winter apples, 1 tsp sugar, salt, vegetables (1 onion, carrot, parsley root, black salsify, leek), seasonings (nutmeg, marjoram, pepper, dill and parsley leaves), salt.

Boiled Bream with Horseradish

Clean and wash the bream, and boil in a salted bouillon of seasonings and vegetables. Carefully remove from the pot, and put on a plate, garnishing with grated salted horseradish mixed with coarsely grated apples and sugar. Sprinkle with chopped parsley and dill leaves.

Serve hot with boiled, baked, or mashed potatoes.

Virti žuvies kukuliai

1 kg fresh fish, 2 onions, 2 eggs, 150 g butter, 5 tbsps bread crumbs, 3 tbsps sour cream, pepper, 1 lovage sprig, 1 carrot, 1 parsley root, 1 leek, 1½ l water, salt.

Boiled Fish Dumplings

Clean, scale, and bone the fish. Grind up the fillets, and add finely chopped onions sautéed in butter, sour cream, bread crumbs, ground pepper, crushed lovage leaves, eggs, and salt. Mix very well so that the result is a fluffy and homogeneous mixture.

Pour the water into a pot, add the fish remnants, chopped vegetables (the parsley, carrot, leek, lovage sprig), and salt, and cook for 20 min. Then into the boiling vegetable bouillon put small (walnut-sized) dumplings made from the fish mixture. Cook for 10–15 min. more.

When done, remove the dumplings, sprinkle with chopped parsley leaves, pouring melted butter over everything.

Serve hot with boiled or mashed potatoes, or if they are served cold, serve them with horseradish or mayonnaise.

Kepti žuvies kukuliai

1 kg zander, cod, pike, flounder, or other fish, 2 slices white bread, 2 onions, ½ cup milk, 20 g butter, 2 eggs, ½ cup sour cream, pepper, marjoram, 50 g bread crumbs, cooking fat, salt.

Fried Fish Patties

Clean and wash the fish, peel off the skin, and remove the bones. Grind up the fillets, and add finely chopped onions sautéed in butter, white bread soaked in milk and squeezed out, eggs, sour cream, seasonings, and salt, mixing very well so that the mixture is fluffy and homogeneous.

From this mixture, make small patties by rolling in the crumbs, and then fry in heated fat until a nice crust forms.

Serve hot fish patties with boiled potatoes and pickles.

Cold fish patties can be served with sour cream mixed with horseradish or finely chopped pickles.

Fish Dumplings with Buckwheat

Žuvų kukuliai su grikiais

½ kg fish, 3–4 boiled potatoes, 2 cups buckwheat flour, thyme, pepper, cooking fat, salt.

Gut, scale, bone, and finely chop the fish. To the chopped fish add mashed boiled potatoes, flour, ground pepper, crushed thyme, and salt, kneading everything together well. From this mixture make round dumplings, flattening them slightly, and frying in heated fat in a hot oven (220 °C) for about 30–35 min., turning over and frying on both sides, until a nice crust forms.

Serve hot, with melted butter poured over the dumplings, along with boiled or baked potatoes.

Fish Patties with Mushroom Filling

Žuvies paplotėliai su grybų įdaru

800 g fish, 2 onions, 2 eggs, 200 g butter, 1 cup bread crumbs, 2 tbsps sour cream, pepper, oregano, marjoram, salt, parsley or dill leaves.
FOR THE FILLING:
5 dried mushrooms, 1 onion, 50 g butter, salt.

Clean, scale, and bone the fish, grind up the fillets, add finely chopped onions sautéed in butter, sour cream, 3 tablespoons of bread crumbs, eggs, ground pepper, chopped marjoram and chopped oregano, and salt, mixing very well so that what results is a fluffy and homogeneous mixture.

To make the filling, soak the mushrooms for 2–3 hrs., then boil in the same water, and slice or chop very finely, adding a finely chopped onion sautéed in butter, along with salt. Mix thoroughly.

Make patties from the fish mixture, and on each of them put a tablespoon of mushroom filling. Then make a round dumpling, and then flattening it. The result is a round patty. Roll the patties in the crumbs, and fry on both sides in butter until a nice crust forms. Then pour the mushroom broth into the frying pan, cover, and stew for another 10–15 min.

When done, put the patties into a bowl, using the liquid in which they were stewed and pouring it over the patties. Sprinkle with chopped parsley or dill leaves.

Serve hot with boiled potatoes and pickles.

Fish Pancakes with Grated Potatoes

Žuvies blyneliai su bulvių tarkiais

400 g fish, 2 onions, 1 egg, tarragon, thyme, 1 l grated potatoes, cooking oil.

Squeeze out the grated potatoes, but do not throw out the liquid, waiting until the starch settles. Then pour off the liquid, and add the starch to the gratings.

Clean, scale, and bone the fish. Grind up the fillets, adding finely chopped onions sautéed in butter, eggs, crushed tarragon and thyme, the grated potatoes, and salt. Mix well. Make little pancakes 4–5 cm in diameter and 2 cm thick, and put into a frying pan with heated fat, frying in an oven for 20–25 min., flipping them over and frying on both sides.

Serve hot with stewed sauerkraut and with pickles mixed with sour cream.

Ground Cod

Menkės maltinis

1 kg cod, 3 slices white bread, milk in which to soak the bread, 2 onions, 100 g butter, 3 eggs, pepper, coriander, nutmeg crumbs, dill sprigs, salt.

Wash, scale, and bone the cod. Grind up the fillets. To the ground cod add bread soaked in milk and squeezed out, finely chopped onions sautéed in butter, two eggs, ground seasonings, and salt. Mix well so that the mixture is fluffy and homogeneous.

From this mixture make a small oblong loaf, and put into a greased baking pan. Apply beaten egg to the surface, and sprinkle with crumbs.

Bake in a moderate oven (180 °C) for 45–60 min.

It can be eaten either hot or cold. It can be served hot with mashed potatoes, pickles, and vegetable salads, or cold with horseradish sauce and vegetable salads.

Fish Cake

Žuvies apkepas

1 kg boneless fish, 4 eggs, ½ kg boiled finely grated carrots, 200 g sour cream, 2 slices white bread, 2 onions, 1 cup green peas, pepper, marjoram, parsley, dill, salt.

Grind up the fish and onions, adding the bread after soaking and squeezing out, 3 eggs, pepper, and salt, mixing everything thoroughly. Put this mixture into a greased cake mould, and bake in a moderate oven (180 °C) for 30 min. When almost done, put the carrots and peas on top, pouring a beaten salted egg over everything, and bake for about 15 min. more.

Decorate with onion rings fried in oil, adding thick sour cream. Sprinkle with chopped dill and parsley leaves.

Serve either warm or cold. If warm, serve with hot potatoes, and with black bread if served cold.

Dried or Salted Fish Casserole

Žuvelių šutinys

1 kg small dried or salted fish, 1 kg potatoes, 200 g sour cream, 100 g butter, seasonings (dill, oregano, bay leaves, pepper).

Soak the dried or salted fish in cold water for 20–30 min. If very salty, soak longer, changing the water several times.

Peel the potatoes, and slice into small (2–3 cm) cubes. Pour a very small amount of water into a pot, and make a layer of potatoes (if the fish are salty, do not add salt to the potatoes). On top of the potatoes add a layer of fish, sprinkle with the seasonings, and then another layer of potatoes until all the ingredients are used. The last layer should be of potatoes. Pour sour cream on top, adding dollops of butter. Bake in a covered pot in a moderate oven (180 °C) for 20–25 min.

Serve with pickled beets, pickles, or sauerkraut.

Žuvelių ir grybų šutinys

1 kg salted or dried fish, ½ l salted mushrooms, 2–3 cloves garlic, 100 g butter, 200 g sour cream, dill, thyme.

Fish and Mushroom Casserole

Soak and wash the mushrooms well. Also soak the fish in cold water (if salty, change the water several times).

Pour ½ cup of water into a pot, making a layer of mushrooms at the bottom, then of fish, making layers until you run out of ingredients. The last layer should be of mushrooms. Sprinkle each layer with the seasonings. Pour sour cream on top, add pats of butter. Cover the pot, and bake in a moderate oven (180 °C) for 25–30 min.

Serve with boiled or baked potatoes.

Žuvis, šutinta su bulvėmis

1 kg pike, tench, zander, catfish, or other large fish, 1 kg potatoes, seasonings (marjoram, bay leaves, pepper, dill), 200 g butter, 200 g cream, salt.

Fish Stewed with Potatoes

Clean and wash the fish, cut into pieces, rub with salt mixed with the seasonings, and let stand for 30–40 min.

Peel and quarter the potatoes. Pour several tablespoons of water into a pot or baking pan. Then put in the first layer of potatoes, and sprinkle with dill, then a layer of pieces of fish, then again potatoes until you run out of the ingredients. The last layer should be of potatoes. After putting in the fish and potatoes, add cream and dollops of butter. Cover the pot or pan, and stew in a moderate oven (180 °C) for 35–40 min.

Serve in the same pot or pan in which this dish was baked, along with pickles or cucumbers, sauerkraut or cabbage.

Su bulvėmis šutintos žuvelės

1 kg fresh small fish (roach, bleak, smelt, perch, or others), 1½ kg potatoes, 200 g butter, 200 g cream, fresh or dried stems of dill with the seeds, thyme sprigs, salt.

Small Fish Stewed with Potatoes

Clean the small fish, and remove the gills. Peel and quarter the potatoes. On the bottom of a pot, put a layer of potatoes, then one of fish, and continuing this order until you run out of ingredients. Salt each layer separately. Sprinkle the seasonings on the layers of fish. The top layer should be of potatoes. Add cream, and also put dollops of butter on top. Cover, and stew in a moderate oven (180 °C) for 25–30 min.

Serve this stew in the same pot in which it was made. Arrange the small fish on the plates carefully so that they do not fall apart.

Virta žuvis

1 kg tench, pike, or other large fish, vegetables (1 carrot, parsley root, leek, onion, ½ stalk celery), seasonings (dill, pepper, bay leaves, tarragon, thyme), 200 g butter, salt.

Boiled Fish

Put chopped vegetables on the bottom of a pot, putting fish cut into pieces on top. Sprinkle with seasonings, and add salt. Pour enough water to cover everything, and cook over a low flame in a covered pot for about half an hour, always watching that the ingredients do not overcook and become mushy.

When done, carefully remove the fish, and put into a bowl. Drizzle with melted butter, and sprinkle with chopped parsley or dill.

Serve with boiled or mashed potatoes and fresh or pickled vegetables.

Virti vėžiai

1 kg crayfish, ½ l beer, green onions, dill stem, 1 horseradish root, parsley root and sprigs, dill sprigs, 3 l water, 50 g butter, salt.

Boiled Crayfish

Pour cold water over the crayfish, and let stand for 10–15 min. (for the dirt to come off). Bring water to a boil in a pot, add salt, pour in the beer, add the green onions, dill stem, parsley root, and horseradish root. Bring to a boil. Put the crayfish into the boiling water, and in a covered pot cook over a low flame for 15 min. Remove the pot from the heat, and keep covered for about 1 hour more so that the crayfish absorb the aroma of the seasonings.

Remove and drain the crayfish, add butter to make them glisten, and sprinkle with dill and parsley leaves.

Įdaryta lydeka drebučiuose

1 kg pike, 1 lemon, seasonings (pepper, coriander, nutmeg), salt.
FOR THE FILLING:
2 onions, 50 g butter, 2 slices white bread, milk in which to soak the bread, 2 eggs, vegetables (1 carrot, celery stalk, parsley root, leek).

Stuffed Pike in Aspic

Scale the pike, slitting open from below the neck. Clean out, wash, and dry. Remove the skin, leaving a thin layer of muscle attached to it. Remove the meat from the bones, and grind up together with the bread after soaking in milk and squeezing out, plus eggs, onions sautéed in butter, ground seasonings, and salt, mixing well so that the mixture is fluffy. If the mixture is too thick, dilute with cream or milk. Spoon the filling into the skin of the pike, and sew up the underside.

After preparing, put the pike into a pot for cooking fish, poke a few holes with a needle, and sprinkle with chopped vegetables and seasonings, and also adding cold water. Cook for about 1 hour. Separately boil the bouillon for the aspic from the head and bones of the pike after adding a little water. To make the aspic firmer, gelatine may be added.

When the stuffed pike is done, carefully remove from the bouillon, and place in a bowl. After cooling, pour the aspic over the fish as it is setting, and garnish with lemon slices, hard-boiled eggs, and greens.

This is a dish for special occasions and major holidays.

Fish in Aspic

Žuvies drebučiai

½ kg pike or other large fish, 1 carrot, 1 parsley plant with the roots, dill, 3–4 peppercorns, 1 onion, 1 bay leaf, salt.
FOR THE SAUCE:
3–4 tbsps grated horseradish, 200 g sour cream, 1 tbsp sugar, ½ tsp salt.

After preparing the fish and putting it a pot (the gills must be removed from the head), pour cold water in the pot until the fish is covered. Add a sliced carrot, parsley, dill, pepper, a bay leaf, an onion, and salt, cooking over a low flame for about an hour. When done, remove the bones, put the pieces of fish into one large mould or into several small ones, and press together. Pour the bouillon over it in which it was cooked in, and let stand to cool.

After the fish has set, turn over onto a plate, garnish with parsley and dill sprigs, along with slices of lemon and boiled carrot.

This dish is made for holidays and special occasions, and served with horseradish sauce made combining grated horseradish, sour cream, sugar and salt, mixing well.

Herring with Sour Cream

Silkė su grietine

3 herrings, 200 g sour cream, 1 onion, 1 hard-boiled egg, green onions, parsley sprigs.

Soak, clean, scale, and bone the herring. Slice into small pieces, put on a plate, pouring sour cream over it. Sprinkle with finely chopped onions or sliced green onions.

Garnish with parsley sprigs and a finely chopped hard-boiled egg.

Serve as a snack with hot boiled or baked potatoes.

Fried Herring

Kepta silkė

3 herrings, 2 tbsps flour, cooking oil.

Soak, scale, and bone the herring. Cut into fillets. Roll in flour, and fry in oil. Make a cut in the side of each fillet to keep the herring from curling.

Put on a plate, pouring the oil in which they were fried over the fillets.

Serve cold with black bread as a snack.

Fried herring are sometimes also served hot with boiled or baked potatoes in the afternoon.

"Herring"

"Silkė"

4 herrings, 2 apples, 2 onions, 2 eggs, 2 tbsps bread crumbs, cooking oil.
FOR THE GARNISH:
radishes, cucumbers, tomatoes, sprigs of parsley, green onions.

Soak, scale, bone, and chop the herring, adding the bread crumbs, finely chopped onions sautéed in oil, finely grated apples, and finely chopped hard-boiled eggs. Mix everything thoroughly.

From this mixture, make a shape like a herring, garnishing the surface with vegetables (radishes, tomatoes, cucumbers, parsley sprigs, and green onions).

Serve with bread as a snack.

Herring with Ground Hemp Seed

Silkė su spirgine

4 herrings, 4 onions, 1 cup hemp seed,
3 tbsps cooking oil, pepper, salt.

Soak the herring well. Scale, bone, and slice into small pieces, putting the pieces on a plate.

Slice 3 onions, put into heated oil, add pepper, and sauté. After cooling off, pour it over the herring.

Prepare the ground hemp seed in the following way: toast the hemp seed in a frying pan together with a chopped onion, adding salt. Toast until they begin to brown. Then pour into a grinder, and grind up. Then pour the ground hemp seed over the herring.

Serve as a snack with hot boiled or baked potatoes.

Herring with Hemp Seed Milk

Silkės su kanapių pienu

4 herrings, 1 cup hemp seed,
2 cups water, salt, a pinch of pepper.

Soak the herring well, remove the bones, and cut into small pieces, putting the pieces into a bowl.

Wash and drain the hemp seed, and brown for 3–5 min. in a frying pan. While still hot, pour into a grinder, and grind up well. Pour the ground hemp seed into a bowl over the herring. Pour hot boiled water over the mixture, adding pepper and salt. Mix thoroughly.

Serve with hot potatoes boiled in their skins or with black bread.

Herring in Beet Brine

Silkė burokėlių rasale

6 herrings, 3 tbsps cooking oil,
3 onions, 1 cup beet brine,
2 tsps flour, green onions, salt.

Soak the herring well, remove the bones, and fry the fillets in oil. Make a small cut in the side of each fillet so the herring does not curl while frying.

When done, put the herring on a plate, and garnish with slices of onion.

Strain the beet brine, bring to a boil, and while carefully stirring, pour in flour mixed with cold brine, adding salt, and boiling for 2–3 min. Pour this liquid over the herring. Garnish with green onions.

Serve with hot boiled potatoes, peeled or in their skins.

Fried Herring with Sour Cream

Keptos silkės su grietine

6 herrings, 4 onions, 100 g butter,
2 tbsps flour, 1 cup sour
cream, ground pepper.

Soak the herring well, remove the bones, roll in flour, and fry in hot butter. Make a small cut in the side of each fillet so that the herring do not curl.

Slice the onions, sauté in butter, and add the sour cream. Mix thoroughly, and heat for 3-5 min.

Put the herring on a plate, pouring the onions over them. Serve with hot boiled potatoes.

Silkės tešloje

6 herrings, 100 g butter, 2 eggs, 2 tbsps flour, 1 tbsp sour cream.

Herring in Batter

Soak the herring well, and remove the bones.

Beat the egg yolks, add flour, sour cream, and well-beaten egg whites. Mix everything thoroughly. Dip the herring fillets in this batter, and fry on both sides in butter. To keep them from curling, make a cut in the side of each fillet.

Serve warm with stewed or baked potatoes.

Silkės su grybų įdaru

6 herrings, 3 onions, 5 tbsps cooking oil,3 tbsps sour cream, 6 dried mushrooms, pepper, sugar.

Herring with Mushroom Filling

Soak the herring well, and remove the bones. Soak the mushrooms for 3 hrs., wash off, boil, and slice into thin strips.

Finely chop the onions, sauté in oil, adding the mushrooms, pepper, and a little sugar. Saute for 5–10 min. more. Spread this filling on the herring fillets, and roll them up. Put on a plate, and pour over with sour cream.

Serve as a snack with bread or hot potatoes.

Silkės krienų padaže

6 herrings, 100 g cooking oil, 100 g flour, 100 g horseradish, 10 g sugar, 3 egg yolks, 1 cup sour cream, several drops of vinegar.

Herring in Horseradish Sauce

Soak and fillet the herring, roll in flour, and fry in oil. Put on a plate, pouring horseradish sauce over the herring.

To make the sauce, sauté the flour in oil, adding finely grated horseradish, and heat for 2–3 min. more. Add the sour cream, and continue heating, sprinkling in several drops of vinegar, a little sugar and the egg yolks after beating with salt. Heat while stirring. After cooling off, pour the sauce over the herring.

Silkių maltiniai su burokėliais

*5 herrings, 4 boiled potatoes, 3 eggs, ½ cup milk, 3 tbsps sour cream, 2 onions, 200 g butter, bread crumbs, pepper.
FOR THE GARNISH:
3 boiled beets, 1 onion, 50 g butter, 2 tbsps flour, 1 tsp sugar, 1 cup sour cream, beet brine or a little vinegar, salt.*

Herring Croquettes with Beets

Soak, bone, and finely chop or grind the herring, adding finely chopped onions sautéed in butter, mashed boiled potatoes, 2 eggs, sour cream, and pepper. Knead well, and make croquettes. Dip the croquettes in a beaten egg, roll in crumbs, and fry on both sides in heated butter for 10–15 min. until golden brown.

Boil the beets, grate on a coarse grater. Finely chop the onion, sauté in butter, and add to the beets. Spoon everything into a pot, adding flour, sour cream, a splash of brine or vinegar, sugar, and salt. Mix well, heating it a bit.

Variously prepared hot potatoes go very well with herring croquettes and beets.

Herring Potatoes

Silkių bulvytės

10 potatoes boiled in their skins,
2 herrings, 2 small boiled carrots,
3 tbsps cooking oil, 1 onion,
1 apple, 200 g sour cream,
1 tsp caraway seeds, pepper, salt.

Soak the herring well, and remove the bones. Fry the herring fillets in oil (raw herring may also be used). Finely slice the herring. Grate 2 boiled potatoes, the carrots, and a raw apple on a coarse grater, adding the herring, a finely chopped onion, pepper, and salt if needed. Mix everything thoroughly.

Peel the other 8 boiled potatoes, hollow out. Spoon in the herring mixture.

Cut the bottom part off the potatoes, stand them up on a plate, pouring sour cream over the top. Sprinkle with caraway seeds.

Serve as a snack.

Smoked Herring Salad

Rūkytų silkių salotos

1 smoked herring, 1 boiled carrot,
1 hard-boiled egg, 1 apple,
3 tbsps sour cream.

Peel and bone the herring, and cut into small pieces. Coarsely grate the apple and carrot, and chop the egg. Mix everything thoroughly, and put into a salad bowl. Pour sour cream over everything.

Serve as a snack.

Smoked Eel

Rūkytas ungurys

1 eel, juniper berries,
cloves, sage, salt.

Gut the eel, rub in salt mixed with chopped seasonings, and keep it pressed for 2–3 days so that the salt sinks in. Then wipe dry, insert little sticks to push the sides apart, and hang it up to be smoked. Smoke for 2 or 5 days, depending on the size of the eel and the manner of smoking – cold-smoking takes more time, while smoking it in a hot place takes less. Finish smoking with juniper branches.

Serve unpeeled and cut into small pieces, garnished with slices of lemon.

Throughout Lithuania smoked eel is considered a delicacy. It is served during holidays and on other special occasions. People who live on the shores of the Curonian Lagoon eat variously prepared eel not only on holidays but also often for breakfast or supper.

Smoked Cod with Stewed Carrots

Rūkyta menkė su troškintomis morkomis

½ kg smoked cod, 3 carrots,
2 onions, 3 apples,
1 cup cooking oil, salt.

Coarsely grate the carrots, slice the onions, peel and core the apples, slicing into wedges. Fry everything in heated oil until the carrots are tender, adding salt.

Bone and finely slice the cod, and put into a bowl. Pour the carrot mixture on top.

Serve with black bread.

eggs

Fried Eggs

Paleisti kiaušiniai

6 eggs, 100 g butter, pepper, salt.

Heat the butter in a frying pan, crack in the eggs. Sprinkle ground pepper and salt on the yolks. While frying, baste with the butter until the whites are completely fried and the yolks are half fried.

Serve with pickles or cucumbers, green onions, chives, and leaf salad.

Serve with bread.

Scrambled Eggs with Hemp Seed

Kiaušinienė su kanapėmis

4 eggs, ½ cup hemp seed, 3 tbsps water, 1 chopped onion, 3 tbsps cooking oil, salt.

Fry the hemp seed in a frying pan together with the chopped onion, adding salt. Fry until they begin to turn brown. Then pour into a grinder, and grind up.

Beat the eggs, adding water, salt, and the ground hemp seed, mixing well. Fry the eggs in oil in a frying pan until golden brown.

When done, serve the scrambled eggs hot with hot potatoes boiled or baked in their skins.

Baked Eggs with Bread

Kiaušinių apkepas su duona

4 eggs, 200 g bread, 100 g butter, salt, parsley leaves, ground pepper.

Cut the bread into small slices and fry in butter.

Put the bread into a greased baking pan, and sprinkle with pepper and chopped parsley leaves. Then add the eggs after beating them. Add salt. Bake in a moderate oven for 20–25 min.

Serve with cucumbers, pickles, and leaf salads.

Baked Eggs with Mushrooms

Kiaušinienė su grybais

6 eggs, 1 cup fresh boiled mushrooms, ½ cup sour cream, 1 leek, 1 tsp chopped oregano, 100 g butter, chives, salt.

Cut the leek into thin slices, and fry in a frying pan with 50 g of butter.

Beat the eggs well, adding the sour cream, mushrooms, fried leek, chopped oregano, and salt, mixing well.

Grease the baking pan well with butter, pour in the egg mixture, and bake in a moderate oven (180 °C) for 20–25 min.

When done, serve the baked eggs in the same pan in which they were baked with finely sliced chives sprinkled on top.

Serve hot with potatoes or bread.

Baked Eggs with Grated Potatoes

Kiaušinienė su bulvių tarkiais

6 eggs, 1 cup milk, 5 medium-sized potatoes, 100 g butter, 1 tsp marjoram, borage leaves, salt.

Beat the eggs. Peel and grate the potatoes, and add them to the beaten eggs. Add the milk, marjoram, and salt, mixing thoroughly. Grease the baking pan well with a thick layer of butter, pour in the egg mixture, and bake in a hot oven for 25–30 min.

When done, serve the baked eggs in the same pan in which they were baked, with chopped borage leaves sprinkled on top.

Serve hot with fresh or pickled vegetables.

Scrambled Eggs with Grated Cheese

Kiaušinienė su tarkuotu sūriu

6 eggs, 50 g butter, 5 tbsps milk, 100 g dried farmer's cheese, green onions or chives, dill sprigs, garden cress leaves, salt.

Beat the eggs well with salt, adding the coarsely grated cheese and milk. Mix thoroughly. Pour a thin layer into a frying pan with heated butter. Fry without stirring over a low flame until done.

When done, make the scrambled eggs into a roll, and sprinkle with finely sliced green onions or chives, dill, and garden cress.

Baked Eggs with Smoked Cheese

Kiaušinienė su rūkytu sūriu

5 eggs, 1 cup flour, 2 cups milk, 200 g dried and smoked farmer's cheese, 100 g butter, 1 tbsp caraway seeds, borage leaves, dill, chives, salt.

Beat the eggs with salt, adding flour, the coarsely grated cheese, milk, and caraway seeds, mixing well.

Pour the egg batter into a greased pan, and bake in a moderate oven (180 °C) for 15–20 min.

When done, sprinkle the baked eggs with chopped greens, and serve in the same pan in which they were baked.

Serve with cucumbers, pickles, and tomatoes.

Baked Eggs with Cheese

Kiaušinienė su sūriu

6 eggs, 5 tbsps milk, 300 g farmer's cheese, 100 g butter, green onions, dill, salt.

Cut the cheese into slices 1 cm thick, and fry in melted butter.

Beat the eggs with salt, add milk, and mix thoroughly.

Put the fried cheese into a greased pan, pour in the beaten eggs, and bake in a slow to moderate oven for 10–15 min.

When done, sprinkle the baked eggs with sliced green onions and dill.

Baked Eggs with Cottage Cheese

Kiaušinienė su varške

6 eggs, 200 g cottage cheese,
½ cup sour cream,
1 tsp chopped lemon balm leaves,
50 g butter, salt.

Beat the eggs with salt, adding the sour cream, cottage cheese (after mashing very well), and chopped lemon balm leaves. Mix thoroughly.

Melt butter in the baking pan, pour in the egg mixture, and bake in a moderate oven (180 °C) for 15–20 min.

Serve with green onions or a leaf salad.

These baked eggs are eaten for breakfast in Suvalkija.

Omelette with a Filling

Omletas su įdaru

6 eggs, 6 tbsps milk,
1 tbsp flour, 100 g butter, salt.

Beat the eggs well, gradually adding the flour while constantly stirring so lumps do not form. Add the milk and salt, and beat well once more. Pour a thin layer of beaten eggs into a frying pan with heated fat, and fry until the surface begins to dry out. Then add the filling, and fold the edges over on four sides.

The omlettes can be made with various fillings:

Mushroom Filling

Grybų įdaras

200 g boiled fresh or dried
mushrooms, 1 onion, 2 tbsps
sour cream, 1 tbsp flour, 25 g
butter, sprigs of parsley
and dill, salt.

Finely chop the onion, and sauté in butter, add the flour. Fry until the onion begins to turn golden brown. Slice the mushrooms into thin strips, and add to the sautéed onion along with sour cream, chopped parsley, and salt, mixing thoroughly. Fry for 3–5 min. more.

Sprinkle the omelette with chopped dill, and serve with hot potatoes and fresh or pickled vegetables.

Cottage Cheese Filling

Varškės įdaras

200 g cottage cheese, 2 tbsps
sour cream, 1 tsp chopped
mint, 100 g butter, salt.

Mash the cottage cheese well, adding the sour cream, mint, and salt. Mix well.

Put the cottage cheese filling in the omelette and pour melted butter over it. Serve with fried bread.

Cheese Filling

Sūrio įdaras

200 g farmer's cheese,
dill sprigs, garden cress
leaves, 100 g butter.

Finely grate the cheese and add chopped dill, mixing thoroughly. Put in the middle of the omelette when it is almost done. Fold over at the edges, and fry for 2–3 min. more.

Serve the omelette hot after pouring melted butter over it and sprinkling with garden cress leaves.

Kiaušinių maltiniai

5 eggs, 2 boiled potatoes,
1 tbsp sour cream, 1 onion,
100 g butter, parsley, dill,
salt, 100 g bread crumbs.

Egg Patties

Hard-boil, peel, and chop 4 eggs. Peel and mash the boiled potatoes, adding 1 egg, sour cream, a finely chopped onion sautéed in butter, and chopped parsley leaves. Add salt and mix well. Make small patties, roll in the crumbs, and fry in heated butter until golden brown.

Sprinkle the patties with chopped dill, and serve with mashed potatoes and horseradish sauce.

Kiaušiniai krienų padaže

8 eggs, 200 g bread, 30 g
butter, 50 g farmer's cheese.
FOR THE SAUCE:
50 g butter, 2 tbsps flour,
1 cup sour cream, 3 tbsps grated
horseradish, salt, sugar.

Eggs in Horseradish Sauce

Slice the bread into small cubes and fry in butter.

Put the eggs into boiling water, and boil for 5–8 min. Remove from heat, pour over with cold water, and peel.

To make the sauce, sauté the flour in butter until golden brown, add the sour cream, butter, horseradish, and salt, heat up.

Put the fried bread into a bowl, and add the eggs sliced in half lengthwise. Pour hot horseradish sauce over everything, and sprinkle with grated cheese.

Serve with boiled potatoes and cucumbers or pickles.

Kiaušiniai su "mundurais"

6 eggs, 100 g butter,
½ tsp green watercress
leaves, salt.

Poached Eggs

Heat water in a pot, and add salt. Break open the eggs quickly into the boiling water. Cook 5 min. When done, carefully remove the eggs, put on a plate, pour over with melted salted butter, and sprinkle with chopped watercress leaves.

Serve hot with bread and fresh vegetables.

Svogūnais įdaryti kiaušiniai

4 hard-boiled eggs,
4 tbsps sliced green onions,
4 tbsps sour cream
sprigs of dill, salt.

Eggs Stuffed with Onions

Cut the eggs in half lengthwise, and remove the yolks. Add salt to the finely sliced green onions, and mix with the sour cream. Fill the egg halves with the onion mixture. Then put the halves on a plate, and sprinkle with chopped dill and crumbled egg yolks.

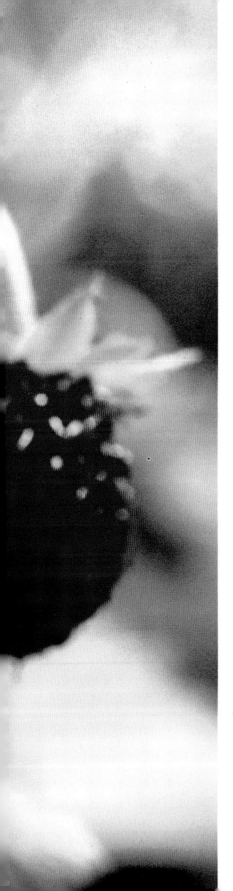

beverages

Caraway Tea

Kmynų arbata

1 tbsp caraway seeds,
1 cup water,
sugar to taste.

Pour hot water over the caraway seeds, and boil for 5–10 min. Take off the heat and let stand for a few more minutes to steep. Pour the strained tea into cups, and sweeten.

Mint Tea

Mėtų arbata

1 tbsp mint, 1 cup water,
sugar to taste.

Pour boiling water over the mint, and boil for 2–3 min. Let stand for 5 min. more. Pour the strained tea into cups, and sweeten.

Linden Blossom Tea

Liepžiedžių arbata

10–15 linden blossoms, 2 tbsps honey,
2 tbsps raspberry preserves, 2 cups water.

Pour boiling water over the linden blossoms, and boil for 3–5 min. Strain, adding the honey and raspberry preserves, mixing well.

Oregano Tea

Raudonėlio arbata

1 tbsp oregano, 1 cup water,
sugar according to taste.

Heat the teapot, add the oregano, pour boiling water over the oregano, and let stand for 10–15 min. to steep.
Strain, warm up, and sweeten.

Thyme Tea

Čiobrelių arbata

1 tbsp thyme,
1 cup water, honey.

Add the thyme to a heated teapot, pour over with boiling water, and let stand for 10–15 min. to steep. Strain and sweeten.
The taste and aroma of thyme can be appreciated better if the honey is not added to the tea, but served in a separate bowl.

Acorn Coffee

Gilių kava

1 l acorns,
1 l milk, sugar.

After gathering the acorns, let them to dry for a few days. Then remove the shells, pour milk over the acorns, and cook in an uncovered pot over a low flame until tender (for about 45–60 min.).
After boiling the acorns, dry well, roast, and grind up.
Pour the ground coffee into a jar, seal tightly, and keep in a dry place.
Use the coffee according to taste (2–3 tsps per cup), spoon into boiling water, boil for 2–3 min., add cream or milk (2 parts to 1 part water), and sweeten.

Carrot Coffee

Morkų kava

½ kg carrots, 1 l water, 200 g cream, sugar to taste.

Peel and coarsely grate the carrots. In a baking pan, spread the grated carrots out in a thin layer, and in a slow to moderate oven (180 °C) dry a little until the colour nicely darkens, but do not burn, otherwise the coffee will have a bitter taste.

Pour the dried carrots over with hot boiled water, boil for 5 min. Take off the heat and let stand for another 15–20 min. to steep. After straining the coffee, warm up, pour into cups, add warm cream, and sweeten.

The carrots can also be dried in advance. They need to be kept in a tightly sealed jar in a dry place.

Grain Coffee

Grūdų kava

½ kg barley, rye, or wheat, ½ l milk or cream, 400 g butter, 2 cups water, sugar.

Dry the grain well in an oven, and grind up.

Put the butter into a frying pan, heat up, add the flour, and while stirring, roast in a frying pan until golden brown. Pour boiling water over the flour, and boil for 5 min. Let stand in a covered pot for 20–25 min. to steep. After straining the coffee, warm up, and add warm cream or milk. Sweeten.

Grain and Carrot Coffee

Grūdų ir morkų kava

½ kg carrots, ½ kg barley, rye, or wheat, ½ l milk or cream, 1 l water, sugar.

Dry the grain well in an oven, and grind up.

Peel and coarsely grate the carrots. Spread out in a baking pan in a thin layer, and dry in a slow to moderate oven (180 °C) until the colour darkens nicely, but that the carrots not burn.

Mix the carrots with the ground grain, pouring boiling water over the mixture, and boil for 5 min. Cover the pot, and let stand for another 15–20 min. to steep. After straining the coffee, warm up, and add warm cream or milk. Sweeten.

If a large amount of this mixture is prepared, keep in a dry place in a tightly sealed jar.

Bread Kvass

Duonos gira

½ kg dried black rye bread, ½ kg sugar, 5 l water, 20 g yeast, 1 cup raisins.

Pour boiling water over the bread, and let stand for about 24 hrs. Then strain, and add sugar, yeast mashed with sugar, mix thoroughly, and keep in a warm place for 1–2 days. Pour the fermented kvass into bottles, putting several raisins into each, and cork well. Keep in a cool place. The kvass can be drunk the next day. Bread kvass can be kept in a cold place for up to two months.

Caraway Kvass

Kmynų gira

½ l caraway seeds, 5 l water,
½ kg sugar, 200 g raisins,
20 g yeast.

Wash the caraway seeds, pour cold water over them, and boil for 25–30 min. Then strain the liquid, add the sugar, and cool off to 35–40 °C. Add the risen yeast, and raisins washed and dried. Keep the kvass for two days in a warm room. Then pour into bottles, and cork well. Keep in a cool place. Drink after 2–3 days.

Barley Kvass

Miežių gira

1 kg barley, ½ kg sugar,
20 g hops, 5 l water,
20 g yeast.

Roast the barley in a frying pan until brown. Put the roasted barley into a pot, pour over with cold water, add the hops, and boil for about 1 hr. After boiling, strain the broth, add the sugar, cool off, and then add the risen yeast. Ferment in a warm room for 1–2 days. Pour the fermented kvass into bottles, cork tightly, and keep in a cool room.

Kvass is most delicious after two or three days.

False Hellebore Kvass

Čemeryčių gira

1 kg sugar, 5 l water, 50 g mint,
25 g caraway seeds, 25 g linden,
blossoms, 25 g thyme, 25 g lemon
balm, 25 g tarragon,
dash of rue, 50 g yeast.

Pour hot water over the mint, caraway seeds, linden blossoms, thyme, lemon balm, tarragon, and a few leaves of rue. Let stand for 3–4 hrs., then boil for 10–15 min. Strain. Add the sugar and risen yeast, and set in a warm place to ferment. When the yeast begins to ferment, pour into an oak keg or into bottles, seal or cork tightly, and keep in a cool place.

The kvass can be drunk the next day.

It is a rather sharp beverage with a distinctive taste.

Hops Kvass with Juice

Apynių gira su sultimis

50 g hops, 1 kg sugar,
2 l apple, cherry, currant,
or other juice, 3 l water,
50 g yeast.

Boil the water with the hops for 15–20 min. Then cover the pot tightly, and let stand for 2–3 hrs. Strain the liquid, adding the sugar and juice. Warm up the resulting liquid to 35–40 °C, and add dissolved yeast. Ferment warmly for approximately 12–24 hrs., and then pour into bottles.

The kvass is ready to drink on the second or third day. It has a sweet-and-sour taste and is rather strong. The acidity and colour depend on the kind of juice used.

Cranberry Kvass

/ 177 /

Spanguolių gira

1 kg cranberries, 1 kg sugar, 20 g yeast, 5 l water.

Put the cranberries into a pot and add water, bringing it to a boil. Boil for 8–10 min. Mash the berries, pouring the water in was boiled in several times over the berries, and strain. After the liquid has cooled off, add sugar and risen yeast, and put in a warm place to ferment for 2–3 days. Serve fermented kvass immediately, or pour into bottles, cork, and keep in a cool place.

Whey Kvas

Išrūgų gira

5 l whey, ½ kg sugar, 2 tbsps chopped southernwood, 3 tbsps chopped sweet flag leaves, 50 g yeast.

Strain the whey, adding the chopped southernwood and sweet flag, and bring to a boil. Let cool, strain, add the sugar and risen yeast, and ferment in a warm place.

Whey kvass can be drunk the next day or kept in sealed containers in a cool place.

Honey Kvass

Medutinė gira

½ l honey, 5 l water, 20 g yeast, 200 g raisins, 2 lemons.

Pour the honey over with hot boiled water and stir until it dissolves.

Let cool, add risen yeast, and ferment for 24 hrs. in a warm room until the kvass begins to foam. Skim off the foam, add the raisins after washing and drying, and add the juice from the lemons. Pour the kvass into bottles, and keep in a cool place.

Honey kvass is made for holidays, weddings, and also for more solemn occasions.

Honey Wine

Medaus vynas

5 l apple juice, ½ l honey, 25 g yeast.

Add the honey to the juice and heat while stirring, until the honey dissolves. Let cool off, add risen yeast, and ferment for 2–3 days.

Serve immediately, or pour into an oak keg or into bottles. Seal or cork tightly, and keep in a cool place.

Honey wine is a holiday drink.

Diluted Honey

Mieštikis

After removing the honey, pour boiled water that has cooled off over the combs, and keep for 3–4 days. Then pour off the liquid.

The result is a very tasty and healthful beverage that can also be used as a sauce to pour over savory cooked porridges, various dumplings, and other dishes.

Beet Brine

Rasalas

1 kg beets, 1 tsp salt, 2 l water, crusts of black rye bread, 2 tbsps caraway seeds, 5–6 juniper berries, 1 tsp nigella seeds.

Wash and peel the beets, and cut into thin slices. Pour boiled water that has cooled off over the beets, adding the seasonings, bread crusts, and salt. Press down. Ferment for 3–4 days. Before using, strain the liquid, and serve before lunch or instead of soup.

Beet brine is a very healthy beverage that strengthens the body. It is especially suitable for winter and early spring.

Cranberry Beverage

Spanguolių gėrimas

1 cup cranberries, 3–4 tbsps honey, 1 l water, 1 tsp sage.

Put the cranberries in a cheesecloth and tie the ends together, immerse in boiling water with seasonings, boil for 2–3 min., and remove. Without untying the cheesecloth, mash with a wooden spoon in a bowl. Once more briefly immerse the bundle of mashed cranberries in the boiling water, remove, and squeeze out well. Remove the water from the fire, pour in the squeezed cranberry juice, add the honey, and refrigerate.

Cranberry Kisiel

Spanguolių kisielius

2 cups cranberries, 2 l water, 200 g sugar, 1 cup potato starch.

Pick over the berries, tie up in a cheesecloth, and immerse in boiling water. Boil for 2–3 min., remove the berries, and mash with a wooden spoon in a bowl without untying the cheesecloth. Briefly soak the bundle of mashed cranberries in the boiling water, remove, and squeeze out well. Dissolve the starch in cold water, pour into the boiling water, and bring to a boil. Add the squeezed cranberry juice, but do not bring to a boil again. Sweeten.

Cranberry kisiel is a traditional dish on Christmas Eve.

Beet Kisiel

Burokėlių kisielius

2 cups beet juice, 2 l water, 4 tbsps starch, 1 cup sugar, vanilla bark, 2 lemons.

Dissolve the starch, pour into boiling water, add the vanilla bark, sugar, beet juice, and juice from one of the lemons. Bring to a boil. Pour into a pitcher, cut the other lemon into thin slices, add to the kisiel, and let cool.

Beet kisiel has a beautiful red colour and a distinctive taste.

Sula Sap

Before the trees are in leaf, in spring at the end of March maples and birches are tapped for their sap. Maple sap is sweeter, and as a result is tapped more often. Drill a hole in the trunk of the tree, press in a sharpened tube or other device through which the sap will drip from the trunk into a container set below. The spile must not be of pine or spruce, as the sap from these trees is bitter. The sap can be drunk fresh or fermented.

Rauginta sula Fermented Sap

Fill a wooden keg with maple or birch sap. For flavoring, add black currants, cherries, or oak twigs. Pour a layer of oats on top. Oats are light, and they will remain on the surface and sprout, forming a cover at least 5 cm thick. In this way, the covered sap will gradually ferment into a delicious sour beverage. Keep sap fermented in this way in a cool room for several months to quench your thirst on hot summer days. In order to draw sap from the keg, use a knife to cut out a circle 10 cm in diameter. Remove the circle, draw the sap with a cup or ladle, and cover again with the same circle.

When sap is fermented, hops are sometimes also added. In the Dzūkija region, sometimes dried apples are added to the mixture.

Aguonų pienas Poppy seed Milk

1 cup poppy seeds, 1 l water, ½ cup sugar.

Pour boiling water over the poppy seeds, and let stand for 2–3 hrs. to swell up. Then pour off the water, mash the poppy seeds well or grind 2–3 times in a meat grinder, add 1 l of boiled water that has cooled off, strain, and sweeten.

Serve poppy seed milk with various pastries and porridges. It can also be used to make soups and various beverages, or poured over oat kisiel and Christmas Eve biscuits.

Midus Mead

Real mead is made from natural light bees' honey (from the nectar of linden blossoms, fruit trees, sowthistles, or white clover).

When mead is made at home in Lithuania and neighboring countries, different flavorings are added.

Lithuanian Mead

Lietuviškas midus

10 kg honey, 10 l water,
10 g dry hops buds,
15 g dried juniper berries,
40 g cultured wine yeast.

Put the honey into a clean enamel pot, then adding pure drinking water (preferably from a spring) in the pot. Mix thoroughly and heat over a low flame. When the water comes to a boil, immerse a clean cheesecloth bag with the flavorings by a string in the pot. Boil, removing the foam until the liquid stops foaming, which takes about half an hour.

Cool the boiled liquid down to a temperature of 30 °C, add the yeast, and pour into a large glass bottle (20–25 l). Tightly seal the bottle with a boiled cork that has a hole in it. Insert a small hose or a bent glass tube into the hole. Put the other end of the tube into a bottle of water. The gases that appear during fermentation will escape through the water. Keep the bottle for 2–3 weeks in a warm room (22–25 °C).

When the fermentation has slowed, and lees have appeared at the bottom of the bottle, carefully pour the mead, leaving the lees, into another bottle. Seal this bottle also and keep for 2–3 months at the same temperature. Then pour out the mead a second time, pour into an oak keg, seal tightly, and age in a cool room. Strong mead is aged for 4–5 years, and even as long as 10 years.

When making dry mead, one that is weak or of medium strength, dilute 1 kg of honey with 2–3 liters of water. This type of mead ages more quickly.

Weak Mead

Silpnas midus

3 kg honey, 10 l water,
50 g dry hops buds, 40 g yeast.

Boil and prepare in the same way as strong mead, only do not pour into a special bottle, but ferment in a container covered with cheesecloth at a temperature of 22–25 °C for 1–2 weeks. Then strain, pour into an oak keg, seal tightly, and put in a cool room for 3–4 weeks. Mead that has been kept for a longer period has a better taste.

Holiday Spirit

Šventinė

3 tbsps honey,
3 tbsps caraway seeds,
½ l homemade vodka.

Boil the caraway seeds in a small amount of water for 5–10 min. Let cool, and strain. Pour the liquid back into the pot in which it was boiled, and heat over a low flame. While constantly stirring, add the honey and vodka. Heat to boiling, but do not boil. Let cool, and pour into a bottle or special container.

It is a beverage for the big holidays of Christmas and Easter. It is especially popular in the Dzūkija region.

baked goods
and sweet dishes

Wedding Cake

Svočios karvojus

*1½ kg flour, 1½ cups milk,
150 g yeast, 10 egg yolks,
400 g butter, 400 g sugar,
3 cups raisins, 1 packet
vanilla sugar, salt.
FOR THE ICING:
3 egg whites, 3 cups
powdered sugar.*

Warm the milk, add crumbled yeast, half of the sugar, ½ kg of flour, mix thoroughly, and set aside to rise.

To the risen yeast, add the egg yolks after mixing with sugar, melted and cooled butter, the rest of the flour, the vanilla sugar, and some salt. Knead the dough until little white bubbles appear on the surface. Toward the end of kneading, add the raisins after washing and drying them. Cover the dough warmly, and let rise in a warm place for 1–1½ hrs.

After the dough has risen, make one big round cake, put into a round greased baking pan, and let rise for about another hour.

After the cake has risen, put a strip braided from two or three strands of dough around the edges, and on top press circles with a glass. Insert plenty of toothpicks dipped in egg white.

Bake in a hot oven for about an hour and a half. When done, apply egg white to the cake, and let cool. After cooling, decorate: remove the toothpicks that were inserted, and in their place stick shapes of little birds, animals, and stars baked from the dough, and apply white icing or sprinkle with powdered sugar. When taking the cake to a wedding, put rue and other flowers into the holes that were made with the toothpicks.

Karvojus is a ceremonial wedding cake.

Wedding Ring Cake

Vestuvinė riestė

*1 kg flour, 100 g yeast,
1 cup milk, 5 egg yolks,
300 g sugar, 300 g butter,
2 cups raisins, vanilla sugar, salt.
FOR THE ICING:
3 egg whites, 3 cups powdered
sugar, juice of 1 lemon.*

Warm the milk, add crumbled yeast, 100 g of sugar, and a third of the flour, mix thoroughly, and put aside to rise.

After the yeast has risen, add the egg yolks after mixing with the rest of the sugar, melted butter that has cooled, flour, vanilla sugar, and some salt. Knead the dough until little white bubbles appear on the surface. Toward the end of kneading, add the raisins after washing and drying. Cover the dough warmly, and let rise in a warm place for 1–1½ hrs.

After the dough has risen, make a ring cake (in the shape of an eight), and put into a greased baking pan. To keep the loops from disappearing as the dough rises, put greased heat-resistant bowls in them. Let the ring cake rise (for about 30 min.), and bake in a moderate oven (180 °C) for about an hour.

When done, let the ring cake cool off in the baking pan. Remove from the baking pan, apply a thick layer of icing made by mixing well the egg whites, powdered sugar, and lemon juice.

The ring cake is a traditional cake for weddings. It has been a long-standing tradition for, this wedding cake to be decorated with cut flowers, such as rue and viburnum berries. In the loops of the cake, the matron of honor sets bottles of sweet drinks decorated with ribbons and flowers.

Holiday Cake

Šventinis pyragas

*1 kg flour, 1½ cups milk,
20 g yeast, 10 g salt,
60 g sugar, 100 g butter,
3 eggs, 1 packet vanilla sugar.*

Warm the milk, and add the yeast after dissolving with some of the sugar. Add half of the flour, and mix thoroughly. Sprinkle the surface of the dough with a thick layer of flour, cover warmly, and leave in a warm place to rise (at room temperature the dough rises in 2–3 hrs.). After the dough has risen, add the remaining flour, salt, and the yolks of the eggs after mixing with the remaining sugar. While finishing kneading, add melted butter, vanilla sugar, and beaten egg whites. After kneading a little longer, when air bubbles appear in the dough and it no longer sticks to your hands, even out the surface, cover warmly, and keep in a warm place until it rises again. Then put into a greased baking pan, let rise well once more, spread egg on it, and bake for about 1 hr.

Poppy Seed Cake

Pyragas su aguonomis

*1 kg flour, 1½ cups milk,
50 g yeast, 4 egg yolks,
1 egg, 100 g sugar, salt.
FOR THE FILLING:
300 g poppy seeds,
150 g sugar, 1 egg, 50 g nuts,
1 packet vanilla sugar.*

Combine a third of the flour indicated in the recipe with warmed milk to make a medium for the yeast. Add the yeast after dissolving in milk with one tablespoon of sugar. Sprinkle the bowl of yeast dough with flour, cover with a towel, and leave in a warm place for 2 hrs. to rise. After the dough has risen, add the remaining flour, salt, and egg yolks mixed with sugar, and knead vigorously for 30–45 min. Cover the dough, and again keep in a warm place to rise.

Wash the poppy seeds well, and soak in hot water (for 2–3 hrs.) so that they swell up. Then pour off the water, and drain the poppy seeds well. Finely chop the nuts. Mix the egg with the sugar, add the poppy seeds, nuts, and vanilla sugar. Mixing thoroughly.

After the dough has risen, divide into two parts. Roll each piece into a layer 1–2 cm thick, evenly apply the poppy seed mixture, but do not cover the 1 cm wide strip along the edges. Carefully roll up, put the rolls into a prepared baking pan with their seams on the bottom. Leave in a warm place to rise. Before baking, apply egg to the rolls. Bake in a moderate oven (180 °C) for 40–50 min.

When done, cover the rolls with a towel so that they do not become dry as they cool off. When no longer warm, remove from the baking pan.

On a plate, cut into slices 2 cm thick.

Meduolis # Honeycake

Honeycakes are baked with natural honey. After they have been baked, they should be dark. This colour is obtained by boiling the honey or adding caramelized sugar.

To make the dough fluffy, add butter, sour cream, or soured milk; to make it rise, soda should be added.

Honeycakes are flavored by adding large amounts of different spices. Their taste depends on how much and what kinds are used. Each person baking chooses the spices he or she likes. Usually, they are added in the following measurements: 30 g cinnamon, 30 g ground allspice, 20 g ground cloves, 15 g ground orange peel, 20 g ginger. One can find soft and hard honeycakes baked in Lithuania. Honeycakes have a special quality: when kept for a long time, they not only do not lose their flavor but become even more delicious.

Šventiniai meduoliai

½ kg flour, 2 egg yolks,
1 egg, 50 g butter, 200 g honey,
200 g sugar, 1 tsp soda,
2 tbsps sour cream,
2 tsps mixed spices.
FOR THE ICING:
20 g powdered sugar,
1 egg white, ¼ tsp citric
acid, cocoa powder.

Holiday Honeycakes

Fry the sugar in a frying pan until well caramelized.

Put all the ingredients indicated in the recipe into a bowl, and knead for a long time. The dough should be stiff. After kneading, refrigerate the dough.

From half the dough make little patties or caps shaped like half a walnut, and in each make a small indentation with your finger. Put the caps into a baking pan with their indentation facing downward.

From the other half of the dough make little rolls the thickness of a finger and 3–4 cm long, put into the baking pan, and bake in a slow to moderate oven for 25–30 min.

To make the icing, combine the egg white with sifted powdered sugar. While finishing stirring, add the citric acid.

After baking, while the mushroom stems are still warm, glue to the caps with the icing. Put white icing on the mushroom stems. Add cocoa powder to the remaining icing, mix well, and spread on the caps.

Keep the iced mushrooms in a warm oven for 15 min. more so that the icing dries.

Use the same dough to make honeycakes of various shapes, such as figures of animals and birds, or after rolling into a thin layer, cut out shapes with special cookie cutters. The honeycakes can be decorated in various ways.

These honeycakes are not only baked at home for holidays, but they can also be found at traditional fairs where they are bought as treats for those who stayed at home.

Soft Honeycake

Minkštas meduolis

½ kg honey, ½ kg flour,
3 eggs, 1 cup sour cream,
100 g butter, 100 g sugar,
1 tsp soda, 2 tsps mixed spices.

Boil the honey over a low flame, and let cool. Then add egg yolks mixed with sugar, melted and cooled butter, sour cream beaten with soda, flour, and spices. Beat the batter well. After beating, fold beaten egg whites into the mixture. Pour the batter into a baking pan lined with parchment paper or into various figure moulds.

Bake honeycake in a slow to moderate oven for 30–45 min. When done, let cool. Remove from the baking pan, and slice into small pieces. If baked in individual moulds, then remove carefully without slicing it.

Christmas Eve Biscuits

Kūčiukai

½ kg flour, 1 cup milk,
50 g cooking oil, 20 g yeast,
2 tbsps poppy seeds,
100 g sugar, salt.

Warm the milk, add yeast mashed with sugar, half of the flour, and mix thoroughly. Sprinkle the surface of the dough with flour, cover warmly, and leave in a warm place for an hour to rise. Then beat the dough, add the remaining flour, oil, scalded poppy seeds, and salt. Knead for 25–30 min. until little air bubbles appear in the dough and it no longer sticks to your hands. Cover, and keep in a warm place for about an hour until it rises.

After the dough has risen, make rolls 1 cm in diameter, slice into pieces 1 cm long, and put into a baking pan sprinkled with flour. Bake in a moderate oven until golden brown.

These biscuits are a ceremonial food and are baked only for Christmas Eve. They are served with poppy seed or hemp seed milk. Other names for kūčiukai include šliuželiai, šliužiukai, šližikai, and perpeliai.

Rye Buns

Ruginės bandelės

½ kg rye flour, 100 g butter,
30 g yeast, 4 eggs, 100 g sugar,
3 tbsps caraway seeds.

Put the butter into a bowl, and mash well with a wooden spoon. Then mix in an egg and a tablespoon of sugar, and keep doing so until 3 eggs and 3 tablespoons of sugar have been added. After mixing the butter well with the eggs, add the flour. Afterwards add yeast dissolved in a very small amount of water, and knead well. Keep the dough in a warm place until it rises. After it has risen, roll the dough into a layer about 1 cm thick, spread egg on it, sprinkle with sugar and caraway seeds, and with a small glass (3 cm in diameter) press out round buns. Put into a greased baking pan, and leave in a warm place to rise. After the dough has risen, bake the buns in a moderate oven for 20–25 min.

Rye buns are very tasty when fresh. Serve with tea, coffee, or hot milk with honey.

Dzūkiškas grikinis pyragas

*1 kg buckwheat flour, ½ l cream or milk,
50 g yeast, 2 eggs, 100 g butter,
1 cup sugar, salt.*

Dzūkų Buckwheat Cake

Mash the butter well with a wooden spoon in an earthenware bowl, and while constantly stirring, gradually add the cream or milk beaten with the eggs, flour, yeast mixed with the sugar, and salt. Beat until a fluffy mixture forms. Put into a greased baking pan, and put into a warm place to rise (for 50–60 min.). Then bake for about 1 hr. in a moderate oven (180 °C).

Buckwheat cake tastes good only while fresh, as it quickly becomes stale.

Pyragėliai su grybais

*1 kg flour, 2 cups milk, 25 g yeast,
50 g sugar, 100 g butter, 1 egg, salt.
FOR THE FILLING:
½ l boiled fresh or dried
mushrooms, 50 g cooking
oil or butter, 2 onions,
2 tbsps bread crumbs,
1 tsp lemon balm.*

Mushroom Buns

Warm the milk, add the yeast after dissolving with sugar in a small amount of water, and also half of the flour, and mix thoroughly. Sprinkle the surface of the dough with a thick layer of flour, cover warmly, and leave in a warm place for 2 hrs. to rise. Beat the dough, adding the remaining flour, melted butter, and add salt. Knead for about 30 min. until little air bubbles appear in the dough and it no longer sticks to your hands. Cover, and keep in a warm place for about an hour until the dough rises.

To make the filling, finely chop the onions, sauté in oil or butter, adding finely sliced mushrooms, and sauté for 3–5 min. more. Add the bread crumbs and chopped lemon balm leaves, and sauté for 3 min. more.

After the dough has risen, roll into a layer 1 cm thick, and with a glass press out little circles, putting a teaspoon of the mushroom filling in the middle of each one. Fold over the circles, firmly squeeze the edges together, and put into a baking pan. Let the buns continue rising (for 25–30 min.). After the buns have risen, apply egg and bake in a moderate oven until golden brown (for about 25 min.).

You can serve these buns while they are still hot or after they have cooled off.

Šventiniai kukulaičiai

*1 kg coarsely ground rye or barley,
flour, 200 g honey, water.*

Holiday Biscuits

Knead the flour, honey, and a small amount of water into a stiff dough. Let stand for 4–5 hrs. Put small lumps of this dough on a cabbage leaf or cookie sheet, and bake in a moderate oven until golden brown.

After they have cooled off, the holiday biscuits can be served with hot milk, tea, or coffee.

This is a very old holiday food in eastern Lithuania. Biscuits made with honey were an indispensable part of holidays such as Christmas, Easter, Pentecost, and St. John's Day.

Šventinė boba

15 egg yolks, 250 g sugar, 2 cups milk, 100 g yeast, 200 g butter, 200 g sour cream, 200 g raisins, 5 cups flour, 1 packet vanilla sugar, bread crumbs, salt.
FOR THE ICING:
3 egg whites, 3 cups powdered sugar, juice of 1 lemon, 200 g butter, 100 g chocolate, 200 g hazelnuts.

Holiday Babka

Warm the milk, add mashed yeast, 100 g of sugar, and 1 cup of flour. Beat, cover warmly, and leave to rise for 30–45 min.

Mix the egg yolks thoroughly with the remaining sugar.

Pour all the remaining flour into a bowl, add the risen yeast, along with mixed egg yolks, butter that is warm but not melted, raisins washed and dried, vanilla sugar, sour cream, and salt. Beat everything very well. The batter should be somewhat softer than for a cake. Cover the batter warmly, and let rise for 1–2 hrs. After it has risen, beat well once more, and let it continue rising.

After the batter has risen, pour into a greased mould sprinkled with bread crumbs. (Special moulds are usually used. Their height varies from 60 to 90 cm. The bottom is wider, the top narrower.) The batter should take up only a third of the mould, as the batter will rise in the mould. After the batter has risen, bake in a moderate oven for about 1 hr.

To make the icing, thoroughly mix the egg whites, powdered sugar, and lemon juice. Melt the butter over a low flame, add the chocolate, and melt into the butter.

Remove the babka from the oven, let cool, carefully remove from the mould, and decorate. First, spread the white icing on the babka. Then on top pour the chocolate (after cooling off a little) so that little streams of chocolate easily run down the sides to the bottom. Sprinkle with chopped nuts.

Babka is a holiday cake. Formerly occasions like Easter, weddings, and other various events were not celebrated without it.

There are various kinds of babka, such as bread, marble, hot water, fruit, and others. Each has different ingredients added to the batter.

Aguonų sausainiukai

½ l poppy seeds, 3 eggs, 1 cup flour, 2 tbsps sour cream, 2 tbsps butter, ½ tsp soda, a dash of vanillin, salt, 3 tbsps powdered sugar for sprinkling.

Poppy Seed Cookies

Scald the poppy seeds with boiling water, drain on a sieve, and mash or grind twice with a meat grinder. To the ground poppy seeds, add the eggs, sour cream beaten with soda, melted (but not hot) butter, flour, a dash of vanillin, and a little salt. Beat well. Put spoonfuls of batter (be careful to keep them from running together) into a baking pan lined with parchment paper. Bake in a moderate oven (180 °C) until golden brown (for 20–25 min.). After removing, sprinkle the cookies with powdered sugar.

Šventinės spurgos

1 kg flour, 2 cups milk,
100 g yeast, 8 egg yolks,
200 g sugar, 25 g spirits, 5 g salt,
10 g vanilla sugar, 2 tbsps
sugar, 150 g powdered sugar for
sprinkling, butter, cooking fat.

Holiday Doughnuts

Mix some dough from warmed milk and a third of the flour. Add yeast mashed with sugar, and mix thoroughly. Cover the dough with a towel, and let rise for half an hour. While the dough is rising, beat the egg yolks, adding salt. After the dough has risen, add the beaten egg yolks, melted butter, spirits, the remaining flour, and vanilla sugar, kneading well. Knead for a long time until the dough no longer glistens. Cover the dough with a towel, and let rise for about another hour.

From the risen dough, make walnut-sized doughnuts, put on the towel, and allow to continue rising.

When the doughnuts have risen, put into heated fat. If a small piece of dough immediately sizzles and floats up to the surface when put into the pot, the fat is hot enough. First, fry one side until golden brown, then – the other. Do not flip over again. The doughnuts should be done frying in 7–8 min.

When done, remove with a slotted spoon, put into a colander, and while still hot, sprinkle with powdered sugar.

Narstytiniai

½ kg flour, 100 g butter,
6 egg yolks, 2 eggs,
30 g sugar, 1 cup sour cream,
25 g spirits, vanilla sugar,
cooking fat, 150 g powdered
sugar for sprinkling.

Crullers

To the flour add melted butter, 6 separated egg yolks and 2 eggs with their whites, the sugar, sour cream, spirits, and vanilla sugar. Knead everything. On a board beat the dough with a rolling pin, constantly folding over until little bubbles appear. The more air there is in the dough, the more crumbly the crullers will be. After kneading, cover the dough with a towel, and put into a refrigerator for 2 hrs. to chill.

After chilling, roll the dough into sheets 2 mm thick, slice into ribbons 10–12 cm long and 2–3 cm wide, slit through the middle, and stick one end of the ribbon through the hole.

Heat the fat in a broad, low pot. Add a couple of slices of raw potato so that the fat does not foam up. If a cruller immediately sizzles and rises when put into the pot, the fat is hot enough. When one side turns golden brown, turn the cruller over.

When done, remove with a slotted spoon, drain in a colander, and while still hot, sprinkle with powdered sugar.

These crullers are also called žagarėliai (sticks).

Wild Strawberries with Cream

Žemuogės su grietinėle

1 l wild strawberries,
½ l cream, 2–3 tbsps honey.

Put the fresh wild strawberries into a bowl, and pour over with cream in which the honey has been dissolved.

Serve with black or white bread or with cake.

Other wild or garden berries can be used in place of the wild strawberries, among them berries like garden strawberries, blueberries, raspberries, currants, gooseberries, and cherries.

Bird Cherries with Cream

Ievų uogos su grietinėle

½ l bird cherries,
½ l cream.

Put the berries into a bowl, cover with a plate, and shake well, pouring the cream over them. Serve immediately.

Fresh Berries with Cottage Cheese

Šviežios uogos su varške

200 g cottage cheese, 100 g sour cream, 1 cup fresh berries, 50 g sugar, mint leaves.

Mash the cottage cheese well with the sour cream, mint, and sugar. Heap the mixture on a plate. Put any kind of fresh wild or garden berries on the cottage cheese. A mixture of blueberries and wild strawberries with cottage cheese is a wonderful-looking and also very tasty decoration.

Berries with Bread

Čiulkinys

½ l any kind of wild or garden berries, 100 g black bread without the crust, ½ cup sugar or 2–3 tbsps honey.

Break up the bread into a bowl, add the berries and sugar or honey, and mash with a wooden pestle into a pulpy mixture.

This dish is one that children not only like to eat but also enjoy making. Serve with sweet milk.

Cheese with Honey

Sūris su medumi

½ kg farmer's cheese, 100 g honey.

Cut the fresh farmer's cheese into slices 2 cm thick, and put on a plate.

Pour the honey into a pot, and serve alongside the cheese. Normally the honey is spread on the cheese. Cheese with honey can be served with sweet milk or tea.

Agurkai su medumi

4 cucumbers, 4 tbsps honey.

Cucumbers with Honey

Slice the fresh cucumbers in half lengthwise. With a knife, make shallow grooves lengthwise. Put the cucumbers on a plate with the grooves facing upward, pouring fresh liquid honey.

Honey with cucumbers can also be served in a more convenient way by dicing the cucumbers, and pouring the honey over them.

This is a traditional dish on the day that honey is collected for the families of beekeepers. The family eats freshly picked cucumbers from their garden with freshly collected honey.

Džiovintų vaisių saldainiai

½ l soaked dried apples, pears, prunes, 3 tbsps honey, ground dried nettle powder, dried boiled ground beet powder, dried boiled carrot powder.

Dried Fruit Candy

Finely grind the soaked dried fruit, add the honey, knead, and make little balls 1 cm in diameter. Immediately roll the balls in a mixture of beet, carrot, and nettle powder. The surfaces of the candies will be of various colours and nice-looking.

Spanguolių drebučiai

2 cups cranberries, 150 g sugar, 1 cup starch, 1 stick cinnamon bark, 3–4 cloves.

Cranberry Jelly

Squeeze out the juice from berries that have been picked over, washed, and crushed. Pour water over the remaining pulp, and boil with the cloves and cinnamon peel for about 5 min. Strain the broth, and add the juice. There should be 1 l of strained broth and juice. Add sugar to the broth, and heat up. When it comes to a boil, add dissolved starch, and again bring to a boil.

Pour the cranberry jelly into separate containers, and let cool (until it sets). This jelly can be served as a separate dish for dessert.

Spanguolės cukruje

1 kg cranberries ½ kg powdered sugar

Cranberries in Sugar

Wash the berries, but do not dry. Sprinkle with powdered sugar, and so that they do not rub together, carefully roll in a bowl with the rest of the powdered sugar until a thick, hard layer of sugar forms around them. After rolling, carefully put a single layer of berries into a baking pan lined with parchment paper, and dry in a slow to moderate oven until the sugar hardens.

Serve in the place of candy.

Cranberries prepared in this way should be kept in paper boxes. They can be placed in a dry place for a long time.

seasonings

Daržinis poras

Leek (Allium porrum)
Leeks are grown in vegetable gardens.

They have a very pleasant aroma and a mild taste. As a seasoning, the bulbs and leaves are used to add flavor to various fish and vegetable dishes and soups. Boiled, fried, and raw leeks are used to make hot dishes and salads.

Vaistinė agurklė

Borage (Borago officinalis)
In Lithuania, borage is grown in gardens as a herb and melliferous plant. It has been used in preparing food for centuries.

The green leaves and stems of borage have a pleasant taste similar to cucumbers . Its green leaves are finely chopped and used separately or added to salads. They are especially good in cold beet soup.

Balinis ajeras

Sweet Flag (Acorus calamus)
Sweet flag is very common in Lithuania. It grows along ponds, rivers and in bogs.

The roots and leaves are used as seasonings and have a pleasant smell. Bread is baked on sweet flag leaves. Dried roots or their oil is used to flavor food (canned fish, baked goods, compotes, puddings, icings). Young sweet flag and its rootstocks are chopped and added to salads and horseradish. An aromatic tea can also be made out of the dried rootstocks.

Paprastasis apynys

Hops (Humulus lupulus)
Hops have been known in Lithuania for centuries. They usually grow in forests and in bushes along rivers and lakes. Hops are very often cultivated on farms.

The buds are used after drying. They should be greenish-yellow and still attached to their sprigs. They should have the strong odor characteristic of hops and be bitter. Hops have been used in making Lithuanian mead and beer for centuries. Hops buds are added to bread kvass and other kinds of kvass. They are sometimes also added when fermenting sap.

Kvapusis bazilikas

Sweet Basil (Ocimum basilicum)
Sweet basil appeared in Lithuanian gardens rather recently.

The seasoning uses fresh or dried leaves or a mixture of leaves and blossoms. Basil has a pleasant odor and somewhat bitter taste similar to pepper.

It is used to add flavor to vegetable and cottage cheese dishes as well as soups (especially garden bean) and sauces. It is added to cucumbers and tomatoes when they are pickled or canned. An especially good seasoning for dishes can be made from a mixture of sweet basil, dill, and tarragon.

Paprastasis čiobrelis   # Wild Thyme (Thymus serpyllum)

Wild thyme grows in dry pine forests and gravel pits, along roads, on embankments, and in other dry places.

This herb has a pleasant odor and is added to sauces and soups as well as dairy, cottage cheese, mushroom, and fish dishes. Thyme is used to make an aromatic tea that is not only pleasant to drink but is also said to have curative properties.

Laiškinis česnakas   # Chives (Allium schoenoprasum)

This plant is usually called laiškutis (little leaf).

It grows on damp riverbanks and is often grown in gardens.

Chives sprout very early in spring as soon as the snow has melted, before any other vegetables are growing. For this reason they are prized as one of the first plants of early spring. Chive blossoms adorn flower gardens, and the cut leaves enhance and can be added to fish, egg, vegetable, and dairy dishes. They are eaten alone as salads with sour cream or are added to vegetable salads. Most suitable for eating are the young leaves (before blooming). When they are cut off, they grow back quickly, and after 12–15 days they can again be cut.

Chives have been grown and been used in traditional foods for centuries, and are still popular even today.

Valgomasis česnakas   # Garlic (Allium sativum)

Garlic is yet another vegetable that has been used as a seasoning for centuries in Lithuania. At first, they used field garlic (Allium oleraceum), which they called kiškio cibuliai (rabbit onions).

The heads of the garlic are used for food and in seasonings. Garlic is used not only to add flavor to many foods but also when preserving them (by pickling, salting, drying, smoking, etc.).

Tuščialaiškis česnakas   # Welsh Onion (Allium fistulosum)

In Lithuanian, this plant is commonly called žieminis svogūnas (winter onion).

This very early spring vegetable is grown along the edges of flower gardens, in vegetable gardens, and in sunny places, because it begins to sprout as soon as the snow has barely melted. When cut off, the leaves quickly grow back, and so they are available throughout the summer.

The chopped leaves are used to add flavor to dairy, cottage cheese, fish, vegetable, and potato dishes. They are added to mixed salads or used alone to make salads with sour cream.

Chervil (Anthriscus cerefolium)

Daržinis builis

Chervil grows in forests and bushes, in meadows, in orchards along fences, and in gardens.

Fresh and dried chervil is used to add flavor to foods. It has a pleasant odor similar anise, stimulates the appetite, and enhances the taste of food. Fresh leaves can be added to leaf and mixed salads as well as sandwiches. It goes well with potato and other vegetable soups and with fish, vegetable, egg, and cottage cheese dishes.

Onion (Allium cepa)

Valgomasis svogūnas

The onion is a very old vegetable whose leaves and round tubers are eaten. Wild onions grow in poor soil without the help of planting. Lithuanians began growing onions in the 12th and 13th centuries. This is the main vegetable used as a seasoning in Lithuania. It is added to salads, fish dishes, sauces, and soups. Onions can be eaten fresh, boiled, fried, stewed, or dried.

Garden Thyme (Thymus vulgaris)

Vaistinis čiobrelis

This herb is grown in flower gardens.

It is used as a seasoning both fresh and dried. It has a strong but pleasant odor and somewhat bitter taste. Thyme is good for adding to fish, mushroom, and cottage cheese dishes as well as various sauces. It is especially suitable for adding to pea and garden bean soups.

Garden thyme can be used instead of marjoram, and when mixed with savory, it can be used instead of pepper.

Field Pennycress (Thlaspi arvense)

Dirvinė čiužutė

This plant grows in fields, vegetable gardens, unused land, and elsewhere as a weed. Pennycresses produce a great number of seeds. Their taste has a hint of garlic. For this reason, the pennycress is sometimes called česnakinė (from česnakas, the Lithuanian word for garlic).

In Lithuania, especially in the southern part of the country, the seeds of the field pennycress are widely used as a seasoning instead of garlic.

White Mustard (Sinapis alba)

Baltoji garstyčia

White mustard is grown in flower and vegetable gardens.

The seeds are suitable for preparing marinades and adding flavor to dishes. They are made into a puree that is served with hot dishes and are used to add variety to sauces. In early spring, young mustard leaves are added to various salads.

Southernwood (Artemisia abrotanum)

Diemedis

The Lithuanian name diemedis also has the alternate forms dievo medis and dievmedis. This is an adornment of the traditional flower garden, and is very fragrant.

Young shoots and leaves are used to add flavor to baked goods and beverages.

In the Žemaitija region, the leaves are added to cottage cheese and sour cream dishes.

Elecampane (Inula helenium)

Didysis debesylas

Elecampane is grown in flower gardens and along houses.

The rootstocks are used. They are dug up in autumn, cleaned, washed, cut into small pieces, and used fresh or dried.

They can be added instead of ginger to baked and sweet dishes and used to flavor liqueurs and vodka.

Summer Savory (Satureja hortensis)

Darželinis dašis

Summer savory grows well in vegetable and flower gardens.

It is used both fresh and dried. It is very suitable for adding to garden bean and pea soups and other legumes as well as salads and fish dishes. Very little of this herb should be added, and only at the end of cooking, because if cooked longer, the food will become a bit bitter.

Summer savory goes well with dill.

Lovage (Levisticum officinale)

Vaistinė gelsvė

Lovage is grown in vegetable and flower gardens.

The leaves, roots, and seeds are used as a seasoning. The leaves have a strong odor similar to celery.

Either fresh or dried, the herb and roots are very suitable for adding flavor to fish and vegetable dishes, soups, sauces, and various vegetables.

Hyssop (Hyssopus officinalis)

Vaistinis yzopas

Also called juozažolė (Joseph herb) in Lithuanian, hyssop is a rather beautiful plant and was grown in flower gardens for this reason. Today it also grows in the wild.

Because of their pleasant smell and slightly bitter taste, the leaves and blossoms are used either fresh or dried in cooking. They are especially suitable to add flavor to vegetable dishes. They are also used to flavor vodka.

Sėjamoji juodgrūdė

Nigella (Nigella sativa)

Nigella is grown in vegetable gardens, with the seeds of the plant more often used as a seasoning than the other parts. When dried, they have a very
pleasant taste. They are sprinkled on bagels and other yeast breads and are
added when pickling cucumbers and cabbage. They are suitable for flavoring alcoholic beverages.

Kartusis kietis, or pelynas

Wormwood (Artemisia absinthium)

Wormwood grows on idle land, on dry hillsides, and along houses. It is also
grown in flower gardens.

The herb is used. Because it is very bitter, only a tiny pinch is added as
flavoring. This is a good herb for improving digestion.

Blakinė kalendra

Coriander (Coriandrum sativum)

Coriander is grown in vegetable and flower gardens.

The whole fresh plant has an unpleasant smell, but when ripe, the dry
fruits have a pleasant aroma and somewhat sweet taste.

Coriander seeds are added to fish, herring, and vegetable dishes as well
as soups and sauces to improve their taste. They are also added to various
marinades.

Paprastasis kietis

Common Wormwood

It is a weed that grows in various climates. It has a strong and pleasant
smell and a spicy bitter taste. Earlier, it was popular and widely used (especially for improving digestion). This rather forgotten plant has been making
a come-back recently. It is put in fattier dishes and various kinds of salads.
It is especially good when preparing eel. It can be mixed with onions, garlic,
and juniper berries.

Paprastasis kmynas

Caraway (Carum carvi)

Caraway grows wild in meadows and on hillsides.

Caraway seeds are one of the oldest known and most widely used seasonings.

Caraway seeds are added to sauerkraut as well as to vegetable, mushroom, cottage cheese, and potato dishes and also sauces. They are very
widely used when making cheese, bread, kvass, liqueurs, and vodka. They are
used to make aromatic and medicinal teas. Fresh young caraway leaves go
well with various leafy salads and cucumbers.

Vaistinis kietis, arba peletrūnas

Tarragon (Artemisia dracunculus)

Tarragon is grown in vegetable gardens, and used either fresh or dried. The leaves and stem tops are used as a seasoning to add flavor to salads, soups, and sauces as well as egg, potato, and vegetable dishes. They are especially suitable for adding to cottage cheese dishes and is a spice that has also been prized for centuries. Tarragon is added to cucumbers when they are being pickled or marinated.

Valgomasis krienas

Horseradish (Armoracia rusticana)

Horseradish is a popular and long-known herb grown in vegetable gardens. It also grows in the wild.

The leaves and the thick rootstocks, with their sharp odor and taste, are used as seasonings. Chopped and suitably prepared horseradish is served with cold and hot fish, egg, vegetable, and potato dishes. It is used to make sauces and to add flavor to vegetable salads. Horseradish leaves are used as a seasoning when pickling cucumbers or other vegetables.

Paprastasis krapas

Dill (Anethum graveolens)

This is a very popular seasoning grown in every vegetable garden. The stem, branches, and seeds are used.

In summer, fresh dill leaves are used. They are especially suitable for adding to fresh vegetable salads and soups, especially cold beet soup, and are sprinkled on potato, fish, mushroom, and egg dishes. In cooking, mature dill stems are added and then removed when the food is done. Dill sprigs are added to dishes at or near the end of preparation because if cooked for a long time, they lose their pleasant aroma.

Mature stems with all their ripe seeds are essential when pickling or marinating cucumbers, mushrooms, and other vegetables.

In autumn and winter, dried dill seeds, stems, and sprigs are used.

Tea made from the seeds and dried stems and leaves of dill is also popular.

Paprastasis kadagys

Juniper (Juniperus communis)

Usually called ėglis in Lithuanian, the juniper is found in all Lithuanian pine forests and peat bogs, and less often in spruce forests and in mixed and deciduous forests.

Juniper berries are gathered in autumn when they are completely ripe and fall from the bush when shaken. They are used as a seasoning when cucumbers, cabbages, and beets are pickled. They give a very good taste to salad dishes. They are used to flavor vodka, liqueurs, kvass, and other beverages.

Mažoji kraujalakė   # Salad Burnet (Sanguisorba minor)

This plant is found in the flat sandy districts of southeastern and northeastern Lithuania.

The leaves are used fresh. They have a pleasant odor reminiscent of cucumbers. They are suitable for adding flavor to salads, vegetable and egg dishes, and soups.

Kilnusis lauras   # Laurel, Bay Leaf (Laurus nobilis)

Although laurel does not grow in Lithuania, it is imported from abroad and has been widely used for a long time. It became especially popular after the 1930s.

Tikroji levanda   # Lavender (Lavandula angustifolia)

Lavender is grown in flower gardens. It is a medicinal plant and is also used as a seasoning. Usually the blossoms are used, however the leaves are also sometimes used.

Lavender blossoms give dishes a distinctive taste, but they should be used in very small amounts. They are added to sauces, fish soups, and baked dishes.

Kvapusis mairūnas   # Marjoram (Majorana hortensis)

Marjoram has been known in Lithuania for a long time. It is an annual plant, and is one of the best-known and most popular seasonings. Fresh or dried, the herb is used to add flavor to soups, sauces, and vegetable and cottage cheese dishes. Fragrant marjoram tea is also made from the herb.

Vaistinė melisa   # Lemon Balm (Melissa officinalis)

In Lithuania, lemon balm is grown in vegetable gardens and near apiaries. It has a refreshing smell of lemons. For this reason, the leaves are sometimes used instead of a lemon. They are added to various salads and fish, mushroom, and cottage cheese dishes. Lemon balm is well suited for flavoring beverages and brewing fragrant teas.

Pipirmėtė   # Peppermint (Mentha piperita)

Peppermint is grown in vegetable gardens.

As a seasoning, the leaves are used either fresh or dried. They are fragrant and taste like candy. They are used to add flavor to salads, soups, cheeses, and dishes made with milk, sour cream, or cottage cheese. Peppermint is added to various beverages and is used to make special medicinal and aromatic teas.

Sėjamoji pipirnė   # Garden Cress (Lepidium sativum)

Grown in vegetable gardens, this cress is used to add flavor to salads and potato dishes. It is chopped and sprinkled on baked potatoes and other dishes.

Only fresh garden cress is used. If dried or boiled, it loses its smell, taste, and other qualities.

Didžioji nasturtė   # Nasturtium (Tropaeolum majus)

Nasturtium is grown in flower gardens.

The fresh leaves, buds, and unripe seeds are suitable as an ingredient in salads and in vegetable and egg dishes.

Žalioji rūta   # Rue (Ruta graveolens)

Rue is grown in flower gardens as a national decorative plant.

Rue is well known to every Lithuanian. Its fresh or dried leaves and shoots are also used as a seasoning, but in very small amounts.

Rue is suitable for sharpening the taste of various sauces, salads, and mushrooms and of sour cream, cottage cheese, and sandwiches (especially with cheese) and for adding aroma to tea.

Rue also has medicinal properties.

Kvapusis šalavijas   # Clary Sage (Salvia sclarea)

Sage has been grown in Lithuanian flower gardens for centuries.

It has a strong aroma and a sharp taste. For this reason, it is very suitable for adding flavor to leafy dishes. Either fresh or dried, the leaves are added to onion dishes and salads. Sprigs of sage are used to flavor beverages, kvass, liqueurs, and vodka.

It also has many medicinal properties and improves digestion.

Paprastasis raudonėlis   # Oregano (Origanum vulgare)

Naturally growing oregano is more often found in the southern Lithuania. It grows near forests, in bushes, along roads, on hillsides, and in other dry places.

Oregano has a pleasant, subtle aroma and a strong, slightly bitter, and somewhat sharp taste. The taste of oregano is somewhat reminiscent of marjoram. For this reason, it is called perennial or wild marjoram. Oregano is added to mushroom, fish, potato, legume, and egg dishes as well as various soups. When oregano is mixed with marjoram, the result is a mixture with a very good aroma. Oregano is used to make teas, broths, and flavored vodkas, all of which have medicinal properties.

Daržinė aguona   # Garden Poppy (Papaver somniferum)

This plant is grown in gardens. The seeds are used for cooking. Fresh poppy seeds are almost odorless, but when dried or used in baking, they acquire a pleasant nutty taste. They are used as a flavoring for pastries, fillings, and sweet dishes. The seeds are mashed to make poppy seed milk, which is used in traditional foods.

Valgomasis salieras   # Celery (Apium graveolens)

Celery is grown in vegetable gardens.

Fresh, dried, or salted celery leaves and rootstocks are used as a seasoning. They are well suited for adding flavor to fish and vegetable dishes as well as soups and sauces. The stalks and roots are used to make soups, hot dishes, and salads.

Sėjamoji petražolė   # Parsley (Petroselinum sativum)

Parsley is a common herb and grows in vegetable and flower gardens.

As a seasoning, the leaves and roots are used either fresh or dried. They are suitable for adding to soups, to fish, mushroom, vegetable, and potato dishes, salads, sauces and used to sprinkle on prepared dishes.

UAB „Baltų lankų" leidyba
Laisvės pr. 115a–54, LT-06119 Vilnius
http://www.baltoslankos.lt
leidykla@baltoslankos.lt
Printed by UAB „Logotipas"
Utenos g. 41a, LT-08217 Vilnius